Conversation Lessons

the natural language of conversation

Ron Martínez

Language Teaching Publications

114a Church Road, Hove, BN3 2EB, England

Students' Book
ISBN 1 899396 65 9
Cassette
ISBN 1 899396 70 5

© **LTP 1997**

Reprinted 1997, 1999, 2000.

The Author

Ron Martínez, a native of California, has taught English as a Second and Foreign Language to all levels and ages. He has taught speakers of Japanese, Spanish, Korean, Portuguese, German, Italian and many more. He specializes in the development of very useful and practical classroom materials which are based on solid theoretical principles. He is actively involved in teacher development and linguistic research, including the analysis of computerized corpora and natural spoken discourse. He is currently teaching at St. Giles College in San Francisco.

Acknowledgements

The author would like to thank:
Michael Lewis for being an infinite source of ingenious ideas and good sense.
Jimmie Hill for his patience, thoroughness, practicality, and valuable contributions.
Mark Powell for his useful input and help in bringing out the best in the book.
Judy Boyle for being the inspiration for many of the drama-based activities in the book.
Angela Blackwell for her enthusiasm and help with some trouble spots.
Wendy Harry for helping pilot material 2,000 miles away
Kelly Langer for piloting, valuable feedback, endless optimism and helpful support.
Jeff Mohamed for all his personal and professional support and guidance.

Cover Design by Anna Macleod
Illustrations by Jonathan Marks
Photographs courtesy of Zefa Pictures, The Moviestore Collection, and the Kobal Collection
Printed in England by Commercial Colour Press Plc, London, E7.

What is Conversation Lessons?

Conversation Lessons is designed with both the frustrated student and teacher in mind. It is easy to use and very practical. The student will find language to help him or her sound more natural. The teacher will find exercises that are both easy to manage and student-centered.

What is different about this book?

First of all, this book is largely based on a Lexical Approach. This means that the focus is on larger, easily recalled, natural-sounding 'chunks' of language. The language chosen is widely used and is easy to pronounce. Most importantly, the language is put into activities where there are many opportunities to practice, but where there is always a focus: to become a better speaker *in conversation*.

Getting the best out of this book

This book was designed for speaking. However, it is up to you to decide how long to spend practicing. Encourage students to personalize their input. Let the book be just a starting point. For example, if you use a phrase that has not been included, by all means include it! This book was designed to inspire. Be creative! Dream up as many opportunities to practice as you can!

How to use the tape

The accompanying tape is designed to make the dialogues come to life for the student. There are many ways of using the cassette. You may choose to play the cassette first before reading the dialogue, or after, depending on your aims. You can also try 'pause-listening' – a technique where you pause the tape in key places to have the student complete the phrase. It is also a good idea for students to listen to the dialogues later to remind themselves of language they need to remember.

Why the dialogues are the way they are

The dialogues are designed to be funny and interesting, but most importantly, they are designed to put the language being studied in each unit in a natural spoken context. When you first read a dialogue, you may not notice any special language at all. This is what is supposed to happen. After all, in real life we listen for meaning only, not for particular language. In this book students have a chance to do both.

What to do with the exercises

Again, the focus in this book is on speaking. It is not recommended that you spend much time writing things down. When it comes time for speaking practice, however, it is recommended that some time for preparation be allowed for the student. This will help the student reduce the stress involved in speaking in front of others and make for a more useful practice. Feel free to use the activities in a different order if you wish. Also, don't be afraid to have fun!

Students using the book for self-study

Although this book was mainly designed for use in the classroom, it can also be used by itself. If this applies to you, then the only thing that will be different is that you will have to supply the people and situations to practice with. Remember: practice makes perfect.

Ron Martínez, Berkeley, California

CONTENTS

QUESTIONNAIRE

This questionnaire will help you think about your English. What kind of English do you want to learn? It will prepare you for some of the ideas in this course. When you have completed the questions, discuss your answers in the whole class. Do you all have the same opinions?

1. **When you speak English, how would you like to sound? Check as many as you like:**
   a) friendly
   b) formal
   c) neutral
   d) natural
   e) educated
   f) impressive
   g) informal
   h) cool
   i) exotic

2. **When you speak English, do you want to sound:**
   a) like a native speaker
   b) like yourself
   c) foreign with a foreign accent
   d) American but with a foreign accent

3. **What would you like to be able to do in English?**
   a) function at work
   b) — be able to know what to say in almost any situation
   c) make relationships
   d) watch TV
   e) watch movies
   f) have interesting conversations with native speakers
   g) use English on holiday

4. **If you were surprised about something, which of these would you be happy saying:**
   a) Jeez!
   b) Jesus!
   c) Wow!
   d) Really!
   e) You've got to be kidding!
   f) No way!

5. **If you heard really bad news, which of the following would you be happy saying:**
   a) Oh my God!
   b) Oh God!
   c) Oh no!

6. When you meet a friend, what would you say:
- ⓐ Hi!
- ⓑ How are you?
- c) How you doing?
- d) Hey! What's up?
- e) Hey! What's new?

7. If a friend said to you *How are you*, **how would you reply:** VÁLASZOLNI
- a) Great!
- ⓑ Fine thanks, and you?
- c) Not so great.
- d) Lousy.
- e) Not bad.

8. Which of the following statements is closest to your view: ÁLLÍTÁS ... NÉZET
- ⓐ I want to speak perfect English.
- b) I don't mind making a few mistakes – after all, I'm only learning.
- c) I don't care how many mistakes I make – I want people to like me.

9. Each of the following is a typical student mistake. In your view, which is the most serious and which is the least serious:
- a) Correct: As far as I'm concerned, she's the best I've ever seen.
  - Incorrect: As far as I'm concern, she's the best I've ever seen.
- b) Correct: My brother lives in Sacramento.
  - Incorrect: My brother – he live in Sacramento.
- ⓒ Correct: Could I have some more dressing, please.
  - Incorrect: You must give me dressing.

10. Which, if any, of the following would you feel silly saying? BUTA
- a) What are you doing?
- b) What're you doing?
- c) What're ya doing?
- d) What're ya doin?
- ⓔ Whatcha doin?

11. Do any of the following sound too informal? KÖZVETLEN
- a) Do you have any questions?
- b) You have any questions?
- c) Have any questions?
- d) Any questions?
- ⓔ Questions?

12. Which of the following topics do you NOT want to talk about in class?

a)	the weather	h)	homosexuality
b)	food	i)	religion
c)	death penalty	j)	abortion
d)	homelessness	k)	drug abuse
e)	sports	l)	computers
f)	healthcare	m)	your family
g)	politics	n)	holidays

REMEMBERING

Ingrid The Informant

Ingrid arrives late for her appointment with Inspector Gordon. How does he get from her the information that he needs?

Inspector:	Ingrid. You're late. Did you forget our appointment?
Ingrid:	I'm sorry. It must have slipped my mind.
Inspector:	OK, Ingrid. We want you to tell us where Biggs is hiding.
Ingrid:	I'm sorry. I seem to be drawing a blank.
Inspector:	I see. Maybe this will help refresh your memory.
	The inspector gives Ingrid fifty dollars.
Ingrid:	Come to think of it, I do seem to remember something about a bridge.
Inspector:	Which bridge?
Ingrid:	The name escapes me.
	The inspector hands Ingrid another fifty dollars.
	Hmm . . . it's on the tip of my tongue.
	He gives her a hundred dollars.
	Oh, yes! The Bay Bridge.
Inspector:	One last thing, Ingrid. Is there a shipment coming in tonight?
Ingrid:	Now that you mention it, I think there is, but for the life of me I can't remember at what time.
Inspector:	Maybe you need a little inspiration.
	He hands her fifty dollars.
Ingrid:	Wait. It's coming to me now . . .
	He gives her a hundred dollars.
	That's right! There's a shipment coming in at 11:30 tonight.
Inspector:	Thanks, Ingrid. You've been a big help. Remind me to take you out to dinner sometime.
Ingrid:	Your treat?

1 Matching

In pairs, make a phrase by matching the correct words and phrases. Try to do it without looking at the dialogue.

1. refresh your
2. come
3. it slipped my
4. That's
5. to draw
6. for the life
7. it's coming
8. It's on the tip of my
9. Now that
10. The name

a. right!
b. a blank
c. tongue
d. memory
e. to think of it
f. escapes me.
g. you mention it
h. mind
i. to me now
j. of me I can't remember

2 Sorting

Sort the phrases above into the two boxes below. Compare with a partner.

Remembering	Forgetting
1, REFRESH YOUR MEMORY 2, COME TO THINK OF IT 4, THAT'S RIGHT! 7, IT'S COMING TO ME NOW 8, IT'S ON THE TIP OF MY TONGUE 9, NOW THAT YOU MENTION IT	3, IT SLIPPED MY MIND 5, TO DROW A BLANK 6, FOR THE LIFE OF ME Y CAN'T REMEMBER 10, THE NAME ESCAPES ME

3 Dialogue Practice

In pairs, one person play Inspector Gordon and the other Ingrid.

1. Read the dialogue sitting down.

2. Read it while physically acting out the scene.

3. Do it without the script as much as possible, until you feel comfortable.

4. Do it for the class to see which pairs could win an Oscar.

4 Pair Work

Using the phrases above, what's another way of saying:

1. To help someone remember.

   CAN YOU REFRESH MY MEMORY?

2. "At first I did not remember, but after some more thought, now I do."

   (IT'S COMING TO ME NOW.) COME TO THINK OF IT...

3. "I am very close to remembering and saying something."

   IT'S ON THE TIP OF MY TONGUE

4. "I would not have thought of it otherwise, but what you have just said has made me remember."

   NOW THAT YOU MENTION IT

5. "Right now I am remembering."

   IT'S COMING TO ME NOW

6. "My memory right now is failing me completely."

   I'M DROWING A BLANK

7. "It is difficult for me to remember the name."

   THE NAME ESCAPES ME

8. To forget to do something.

   IT SLIPPED MY MIND

9. "I'm trying very hard to remember, but it's not working."

   FOR THE LIFE OF ME I CAN'T REMEMBER

10. "I now remember!"

    THAT'S RIGHT!

5 Where were you?

Many people can remember where they were when something important happened – for example, when they heard the news of the TWA crash. Many older people can remember precisely what they were doing when they heard the news of the assassination of JFK. Have you any memories of some important event? Where were you and what were you doing at the time?

> **AND YOU CAN QUOTE ME ON THAT!**
>
> *"Mothers all want their sons to grow up to be President, but they don't want them to become politicians in the process."*
> **John F. Kennedy**

6 Role Play – Do you have any comment?

Work in pairs with the following information. Prepare alone for a few minutes.

Student A

> You are a candidate for President of
> The United States. Your press agent
> has advised you to claim you don't
> remember a lot of things about your
> past. If the journalist has proof, say a
> little, but do your best to avoid
> answering.

Student B

> You are a journalist trying to get a big
> story. Ask about the following
> subjects. Don't take no for an answer.
> Pursue your line of questioning.
> You know what politicians can be like.

1. **The money for the presidential campaign.**
   Where did it come from? (You have a document with the exact figures.)
   What is the name of the largest contributor?
2. **Stories about when the candidate was at college.**
   Drug use? (Several old college friends swear that the recent statement
   denying any involvement is a whitewash.)
3. **Rumors about a trip to Rome last year.**
   Reports in the Italian Press last year about an affair with the famous Italian
   opera singer Maria Bellini were denied by the Press Office, but there are
   rumors of compromising photographs.

7 Discussion

**Are you the kind of person who remembers everything – every little detail – or can you never
remember anything – even your own telephone number?**

1. What techniques do you use to remember things?
2. How do you remember new vocabulary?
3. How do you remember people's names?
4. Do you ever forget a face?
5. What do you do (and say) when you see someone you know but can't remember their name?
   What if you have to introduce that person to a friend?
6. What is the most embarrassing situation you have been in when you could not remember
   something?
7. Would you ever reply to the advertisement below? Do you know anyone who would / should?

> **HAVE YOU EVER SUFFERED THE AWFUL
> EMBARRASSMENT OF MEMORY LOSS?**
> Forgotten someone's name at that crucial moment?
> Wanted to drop through the floor and disappear?
> Never again let your failing memory fail you in public.
> We run evening sessions which guarantee complete
> success within 4 hours. Enrol now and put all those
> embarrassing moments behind you! Dial 471-7676 – a
> number you won't forget for a course you'll always
> remember.

DECISIONS

Fickle Fernando

Fernando is talking to his sister. What is his problem? Complete the dialogue using the phrases at the bottom. There is only one correct order.

Fernando: I can't make up my mind.

c Mercedes: 1. _____

Fernando: About Adela and Karen. Right now I'm leaning toward Adela. But then again, Karen is also good.

e Mercedes: 2. _____

Fernando: I have mixed feelings about them. On the one hand, Adela has a good sense of humor. On the other hand, Karen has a great car.

d Mercedes: 3. _____

Fernando: I could go either way. On the plus side, laughter makes the relationship fun, but on the minus side she keeps laughing even when we're kissing.

a Mercedes: 4. _____

Fernando: Yeah, but I kind of had my heart set on Adela. So I'm debating whether to break up with Karen or simply not tell her about Adela.

f Mercedes: 5. _____

Fernando: You're right. I think I'm going to go with telling the truth. On second thought, maybe I should just stay with Martha.

b Mercedes: 6. _____

---

a. Then Karen's the one for you.   b. Who's Martha?

c. About what?   d. What's more important to you – laughter or transportation?

e. Tell me what you like about them.   f. I always say honesty is the best policy.

1 Phrase Jumble

Re-write the following in the correct order.

1. toward I'm leaning Adela

   _____

2. I way go either could

   _____

3. I'm go going with to vanilla

   _____

4. mind my I can't up make

   _____

5. But tea also again then like I

   _____

6. I mixed about feelings them have

   _____

7. I heart my on had set food Mexican

   _____

8. On thought chocolate second I'll the have one

   _____

9. I'm whether debating to call her or letter her write a

   _____

10. On side the plus beautiful it's; minus the on expensive side it's

    _____

11. On hand one the we out go can; other the on hand home stay can we TV and watch

    _____

Now go back and underline the part of these expressions which you want to remember.

2 Dialogue Practice

1. Practice the dialogue in pairs.
2. Take turns being Fernando and Mercedes.
3. Practice until you can do the dialogue without reading it.
4. Do it for the class.

3 Cloze

Only one phrase is possible to complete the sentence.

1. Maybe I will, _____ , maybe I won't.
   - (a) but then again
   - b. I had my heart set on
   - c. on the one hand
   - d. on the minus side

2. _____ stay at home or go out tonight.
   - a. I had my heart set on
   - b. on the plus side
   - c. on second thought
   - (d) I'm debating whether to

3. I think _____ buying a new car instead.
   - a. on the one hand
   - b. on second thought
   - (c) I'm going to go with
   - d. I could go either way

4. _____ , really. I like both public transit and driving.
   - a. I could go either way
   - b. On second thought
   - c. I'm leaning toward driving
   - d. But then again, driving

5. I don't know which to choose. Right now _____ the blue one.
   - a. I could go either way
   - b. I'm leaning toward
   - c. I'm going to go with
   - d. I had my heart set on

6. I'll write her a letter. _____ , I'll give her a call
   - a. On second thought
   - b. But then again
   - c. On the plus side
   - d. On the minus side

7. A: Where are you going this summer?
   B: I don't know. _____ .
   - a. I could go either way.
   - b. I can't make up my mind.
   - c. But then again, no.
   - d. On the other hand, yes.

8. _____ , Erik is responsible, _____ , Kristina is responsible and efficient.
   - a. On the one hand, on the other hand
   - b. On the plus side, on the minus side
   - c. On the other hand, on the one hand
   - d. On the minus side, on the plus side

9. A: I thought you wanted to buy the house on Market Street?
   B: Sure I like the one on Market, but _____ the one on Church.
   - a. on second thought
   - b. then again
   - c. on the one hand
   - d. I had my heart set on

10. Well, _____ , it's close to where I work; _____ , it's far away from the beach.
    - a. On the one hand, on the other hand
    - b. On the plus side, on the minus side
    - c. On the other hand, on the one hand
    - d. On the minus side, on the plus side

4 Pair Work

In pairs choose one of the following ideas. Then write the pros and cons in the grid:

1. living together before marriage
2. driving an automatic
3. living in the city
4. being a dog
5. eating out
6. owning your own business

Arguments For	Arguments Against

Using the phrases from the dialogue, tell the class what you think.

5 Role Play – At a Restaurant

Play the following characters, using phrases from the dialogue.

Waiter: You never know what to recommend.
Customer 1:   You're on a diet.
Customer 2:   You're a vegetarian.
Customer 3:   You're on a budget.
All three customers can't make up their minds.

Use this menu. After practicing, show the class. Can you guess which customer is which?

RON'S KITCHEN

SOUP
POTATO LEEK IN A CUP	1.95
TUSCAN BEAN SOUP	3.95
ITALIAN TOMATO	3.95

SALAD
RON'S MIXED LEAF	6.95
ORIENTAL CHICKEN	9.50
SHRIMP RONNIE	8.95

PIZZA
SANTA FE CHICKEN	9.95
PEKING DUCK	10.95
THREE SAUSAGE	8.50

COFFEE AND TEA
COFFEE	1.25
SINGLE ESPRESSO	1.75
DOUBLE ESPRESSO	3.25
CAPPUCCINO	2.50
SPECIALITY TEAS	1.25
(EARL GREY, CHAMOMILLE)	
HOT CHOCOLATE	2.00

PASTA
SPAGHETTI BOLOGNESE	8.95
EGGPLANT LASAGNA	7.95
CHICKEN FETTUCCINE	8.95

DESSERTS
RON'S RUM BABA	3.95
TIRAMISU	4.95
HOT FUDGE SUNDAE	4.50
FRUIT SORBET	3.50
LEMON CHEESECAKE	4.50
DEATH BY CHOCOLATE	5.50
APPLE PIE	2.50

CONVERSATION FRAME 1

Atsuko's Trip to Paris

Tomo: Did you enjoy your trip to Paris?

Atsuko: Well, it wasn't the most exciting trip I've ever taken, but not bad considering I only had a few days.

Tomo: What were the people like?

Atsuko: Well, they weren't the kindest people I've ever met, but not bad considering all the things I had heard about them.

Tomo: And the food?

Atsuko: Well, it wasn't the most delicious I've ever tried, but not bad considering I only ate at McDonald's.

Tomo: And was the weather alright?

Atsuko: Well, it wasn't the the most beautiful weather I've ever been in, but not bad considering it was winter.

Tomo: And the flight back?

Atsuko: Well, it wasn't the most entertaining thing I've ever done, but not bad considering it was a twelve hour flight.

1 Matching

Working in pairs, match the sentences below.

1. Well, it isn't the greatest car I've ever _____
2. Well, it isn't the nicest wine I've ever _____
3. Well, it isn't the most interesting film I've ever _____
4. Well, it isn't the liveliest party I've ever _____
5. Well, it isn't the cheapest restaurant I've ever _____
6. Well, it isn't the most elegant poem I've ever _____
7. Well, it isn't the most intelligent thing I've ever _____
8. Well, it isn't the warmest day we've ever _____
9. Well, it isn't the funniest joke I've ever _____
10. Well, it isn't the easiest class I've ever _____

a. said, but not bad considering I was half asleep.
b. written, but not bad considering I just wrote it.
c. taken, but not bad considering how much I learn.
d. thrown, but not bad considering the guests.
e. tasted, but not bad considering it's American.
f. eaten in, but not bad considering the food.
g. driven, but not bad considering how old it is.
h. heard, but not bad considering you're only five.
i. had, but not bad considering it's winter.
j. seen, but not bad considering it's a documentary.

Now practice the completed sentences with a partner. One person reads the first part of the sentence and the other person completes it.

2 Negative Comments

In English it is common to avoid a very negative word by using *not very* + *a positive word*. For example:

> It's awful.   >   It's not very good.

Change these examples in a similar way:

1. bad   not very _____
2. cold   not very _____
3. rude   not very _____
4. stupid   not very _____
5. slow   not very _____
6. boring   not very _____
7. dirty   not very _____
8. unhygienic   not very _____

3 Rationalizations

In pairs, think of ways of saying the following so as not to upset someone. Check with your teacher and write the answers in the spaces.

1. He's ugly. _____
2. She's poor. _____
3. He's fat. _____
4. His house is small._____
5. He's crazy. _____
6. That city is dirty. _____
7. She's so slow. _____
8. He's stupid. _____
9. She looks old. _____
10. Your room is quite messy._____
11. Our business is failing. _____
12. Your taste in clothes is old-fashioned. _____

4 Pair Work

Work in pairs. Use the model below to have 12 mini-conversations based on the ideas in Exercise 3 above.

A: He's ugly.
B: Well, I have to admit he isn't the best-looking guy I've met, but not bad considering what he was like when he was in high school. I mean, he had so much dandruff, his shoulders looked like the Swiss Alps!

5 Personalities

Study this conversation. It is fairly typical of what many native speakers say.

A: He's one of the worst-looking guys in the school.
B: Well, he's not exactly Tom Cruise.

Fill in the names of the famous people in the following. Then work in pairs and try to say these dialogues in as natural a way as you can. Use the following names:

Elizabeth Taylor   **Carnegie**   **Whitney Houston**

1.   My parents are really tight with money.
     > No, mine aren't exactly called _____ .
2.   My friend Kelly told me I had a lousy voice.
     > Well, she isn't exactly _____ herself.
3.   My aunt was married six times!
     > I know, and she wasn't exactly _____ !

Now try to make up more similar conversations in pairs.

6 Knock-downs

Answer the questions below individually.

1. What painters do you like?

   _____

2. What cities do you like?

   _____

3. What fast-food items do you like?

   _____

4. What sport teams do you like?

   _____

5. What singers do you like?

   _____

Now talk about your answers with the class. People in the class will comment using the following frame.

Well,	he she it they	isn't the	_____ _____ I've ever _____ , but not bad considering _____ .

7 Discussion

Work in pairs and ask and answer the following questions together:

1. Have you ever been to Paris?
2. If you went to Paris, what would you try not to miss?
3. Have you ever been to Rome?
4. If you went to Rome, what would you definitely go and see?
5. Have you ever been somewhere really exotic? Why would you recommend it?
6. Have you ever been on vacation somewhere really awful? Why was it awful?

AND YOU CAN QUOTE ME ON THAT!

"France is a country where the money falls apart in your hands and you can't tear the toilet paper."
Billy Wilder

When you have discussed these questions in pairs, report to the whole class. At the end of the discussion, take a vote on:

1. the best place for a vacation.
2. the worst place for a vacation.

PRIORITIES

The Nitty Gritty

To be effective in conversation, it is useful to be able to make a point, to state a strong opinion. In this unit, you will learn how to tell someone what is most important – in your opinion, of course. Edwin, Rebecca and Kayo are discussing an important decision. Do you think they will get very far?

Edwin:	The bottom line is we have to stop *talking* about going on strike and start *doing* something about it.
Rebecca:	Exactly. In the end, our words mean nothing if we don't act.
Kayo:	The fact is we need to start planning – immediately.
Rebecca:	When you get right down to it, we haven't really made any progress because we only talk about it. We haven't made definite plans yet.
Edwin:	It all comes down to really deciding to do something. We need more than just talk.
Kayo:	If we don't show them we're serious nothing will change. That's the bottom line.
Edwin:	All I know is that we can talk and talk and talk forever but the real test of our determination is what we do . . . . not what we say.
Rebecca:	It's a question of taking action. Some people talk – we *act*.
Kayo:	I agree. What we're really talking about here is the most important decision of our lives. We must act. Thinking about it is useless.
Rebecca:	The point is we simply can't go on working in these conditions. We have to really plan and do something.
Kayo:	It's just like anything else – you'll never know until you try.
Edwin:	Exactly. I say we start no later than next week.

1 Phrase Gap

Fill in the missing words. Use only one word for each example. Write the completed phrases in the space below.

comes	question	fact	end	down	talking
know	anything	line	bottom	key	

1. The bottom _____ is we need to expand our business.

2. It's a _____ of knowing where to put our money and our time.

3. That's the _____ line.

4. When you get right _____ to it there is no bigger market than South America.

5. It all _____ down to diversification and intelligent globalization.

6. In the _____, if we don't do it, out competitors will.

7. The _____ is there is no other company out there more ready than we are.

8. The _____ is to do it now before they suspect anything.

9. What we're really _____ about here is the financial security of our enterprise.

10. All I _____ is that if we don't do it now, we will certainly live to regret it.

11. It's just like _____ else – to get something big, you've got to be prepared to give something big.

Now go back and underline the phrases to do with "Saying what is most important".

2 Matching

The following is a talk given by a teacher to a discouraged student. First try to work out how the teacher finished the sentences. The actual endings are on the next page in List 2. Match them.

List 1

1. In the end, if you don't study

2. All I know is that when you started with me

3. I know you can pass the exam.

4. The bottom line is there's no easy way

5. When you get right down to it, the only thing holding you back

6. It all comes down to how much

7. Even if you don't pass the test,

8. The key is to speak English as much as

9. What we're really talking

10. If you want to learn English, you have to

11. It's just like anything else – if at first you don't

List 2

a. It's a question of learning the right test-taking skills.
b. the fact is you have improved and there's always next time.
c. you won't learn.
d. you want to pass.
e. you could hardly speak a word.
f. to learn English.
g. is yourself.
h. work hard. That's the bottom line.
i. about here is putting in the time that's required.
j. possible and try not to translate too much.
k. succeed, try, try again.

Go back and underline the phrases which mean "The thing that's most important is . . . ."

3 Dialogue Practice

1. Practice the dialogue in pairs.
2. Take turns being Edwin, Rebecca and Kayo.
3. Practice until you can do the dialogue without reading it.
4. Continue the dialogue until all three characters find a solution.
5. Do it for the class.

4 Role Play – The Power of Persuasion

Below are lines that you can use in four different role plays. In pairs, put the lines under the correct title at the top of the next page.

"All I know is I love you and I want us to be together forever."

"What we're really talking about here is your financial future."

"The bottom line is there is no one else who can do what I do as well as I do."

"When you get right down to it we are no better than other animals."

"The key is to respect all living things."

"The fact is people who finish college make much more money."

"It all comes down to how much you really want this relationship to grow."

"In the end there is no other company I'd rather work for. I'd hate to leave."

"It's a question of sacrifice. We must learn to live without meat."

"If you don't marry me, I won't have kids. And if I won't have kids, I don't want to be with you. That's the bottom line."

Role Play 1   Persuading your daughter/son to go to college

Role Play 2   Persuading your friends to become vegetarians

Role Play 3   Persuading your boss to give you a raise

Role Play 4   Persuading your girl/boyfriend to marry you

Now, with your partner, choose one role play. Using all the phrases from this unit, write new lines under the category you chose. Use these lines to make your role play.

5 Debates

Divide into groups and use the motions below to have a debate. Use some of the expressions you learned in this unit.

1. Experience is more valuable than education.
2. Marriage is a ritual whose time has passed.
3. War is sometimes necessary.
4. College is not for everyone.
5. Drugs should be legalized.

LESSON 5

ENCOURAGING

Rick takes a Risk

Rick and Angie are waiters at a Mexican restaurant. Have you ever been in a situation like this?

Rick:	I deserve a raise. I think I'm going to ask him today.
Angie:	Go for it. It's certainly worth a try.
Rick:	But do you think I stand a chance?
Angie:	You stand as good a chance as anyone. There's only one way to find out.
Rick:	I'm scared.
Angie:	Come on, Rick. Just do the best you can. What have you got to lose?
Rick:	My job.
Angie:	No, really. What's the worst that could happen? Just give it your best shot.
Rick:	Maybe it's not even worth it.
Angie:	Well, you never know until you try. Come on – it's a piece of cake.
Rick:	Oh no . . . here he comes now.
Angie:	It's now or never, Rick.
Rick:	(*Clears throat*) Uh . . . . Mario – Do you have a second?
Mario:	If it's about a raise you can forget it.
Rick:	(*To Angie*) Told you.
Angie:	Well at least you tried.

24

1 Phrase Jumble

Put the words in the correct order. Who can finish first? Remember – there's only one correct order.

1. Go it for

   _____

2. It's a worth try

   _____

3. It's never or now

   _____

4. It's piece cake a of

   _____

5. Give best it your shot

   _____

6. Just best can you do the

   _____

7. What lose you to have got?

   _____

8. You try until know you never

   _____

9. There's find to way one only out

   _____

10. What's happen worst the that could?

    _____

11. You chance a good as stand anyone as

    _____

2 Practice

Work in pairs. Paul's friend Abby wrote him a letter recently because she was worried about passing the examination to enter the Police Force. Fill in the blanks with an expression from the exercise above.

Dear Abby,

Thanks for your letter. Why are you worried about passing that exam? Just go
1. _____ ! After all, you stand as good 2. _____ . Sure, I realize that it's a really
difficult exam, and many people don't pass, but you never know until 3. _____ .
This is the last chance you're going to get, though, so it's now 4. _____ . I mean,
what's the worst that 5. _____ ? I can understand that you're worried that you're not
good enough, but there's only one way 6. _____ . It's worth a 7._____ .
Come on! Give it your 8._____ ! I know you can do it. It's a piece 9._____ .
Just do the best 10._____ . After all, what have you got 11._____ ? Nothing
at all.

Sincerely,
Paul

Now go back and underline the phrases used for encouragement.

3 Pause Reading

Now read the letter out loud to a partner, but pause where there is a space and let your partner complete the expression. Take turns.

IT'S NOW OR NEVER.

4 Pairwork

Using expressions from this unit, what's another way of saying:

1. Try it.

   _____

2. Do the best you can.

   _____

3. Your doubts will never be clear until you make an attempt.

   _____

4. No one else has a better advantage than you.

   _____

5. Even if you do not succeed, how much worse can your situation get?

   _____

6. If you succeed there is much to be gained.

   _____

7. You may never get another chance.

   _____

8. It is easier than you think.

   _____

5 Dialogue Practice

1. Practice the dialogue in pairs
2. Take turns being Rick and Angie.
3. Practice until you can do the dialogue without reading it.
4. Do it for the class.

64 Role Play

Using phrases from the dialogue, act out one of the following scenes:

1. Help a colleague who wants to ask a question during a talk at a conference.
2. You are discussing business relations with an American friend who is considering exporting his product into your country. Decide which product.
3. You're a parent trying to get your child to swim for the first time.
4. You're a pilot of a sky-diving company, trying to convince someone to jump.
5. You want your friend(s) to try the chocolate-covered ants on the menu.

It may help to write it down first. After you've practiced a little, let the class watch.

7 Class Questionnaire – What scares you the most?

Think about and answer the questions below individually and then discuss the questions as a class.

What would scare you the most, or make you the most nervous? Why? Try to reach an agreement on which is the scariest.

1. a. Getting married   b. Getting divorced
   c. Having children   d. Not getting married

2. a. Flying   b. Driving
   c. Walking   c. Cycling

3. a. Not getting promoted   b. Changing careers
   c. Asking your boss for a raise

4. a. Dancing in public   b. Crying in public
   c. Speaking in public   d. Singing in public

5. a. Telling a joke in English   b. Speaking English on the phone
   c. Speaking English in a crowd of people

6. a. Skydiving   b. Bungee-jumping
   c. Hang-gliding   d. Deep-sea diving

7. a. Going for a job interview   b. Meeting new people
   c. Meeting your partner's parents for the first time

8. a. Taking your driver's test   b. Going to the dentist
   c. Meeting your ex-wife in your honeymoon hotel

CONVERSATION TABOOS 1

The Parent-Teacher Meeting

You have to be very sensitive when telling someone about a deficiency. You must know how to gently make suggestions and be careful in your choice of words. Something is not right with this conversation. With a partner, decide what should be changed.

Teacher:	You finally came.
Parent:	Yeah. What do you want?
Teacher:	Your daughter is doing miserably in my class.
Parent:	What are you talking about?
Teacher:	Well, I'm extremely worried about her study skills.
Parent:	Give me an example.
Teacher:	Her mathematics abilities are so bad!
Parent:	Oh, I know she's lousy at mathematics.
Teacher:	And she has absolutely no knowledge of spelling.
Parent:	So? Do you want me to sit with her while she does her homework?
Teacher:	Yes. Do that. Also, you must get a tutor for her.
Parent:	No way.
Teacher:	Well, your daughter probably has no future, anyway – so I don't care.

1 Re-write the Conversation

With a partner, re-write the conversation. The phrases below will help you.

*It might not be a bad idea
it's not one of her strong points
lacking a bit in
needs a little work
has a lot of potential
I'm not sure I understand*

*I have some concerns about . . .
I'm a bit disappointed in . . .
you might want to consider
a little weak
could use a little . . .*

Teacher: _____

Parent: _____

Teacher: _____

Parent: _____

Teacher: _____

Parent: _____

Teacher: _____

Parent: _____

Teacher: _____

Parent: _____

Teacher: _____

Parent: _____

Teacher: _____

2 Conversation Development

1. Ask your teacher for more suggestions.
2. Practice the new conversation with script.
3. Practice the new conversation without script.
4. Act out the new conversation.
5. Show the class.

AND YOU CAN QUOTE ME ON THAT!

"Education is what survives when what has been learnt has been forgotten."
B. F. Skinner

3 Role Play

Decide:
1. Who is A?
2. Who is B?
3. Where are they? How old?
4. Finish the conversation and find a solution.

A: *May I go to the toilet?*
B: *No, you may not.*
A: _____
B: _____
A: _____
B: _____

4 Who said it?

Some of the things below were said by a very critical teacher, and the others were said by a father who wants to protect his daughter. In pairs, decide who said what.

1.   She talks too much.
2.   She's a bit on the talkative side.
3.   I was just like her when I was her age.
4.   She's going through a lot of changes.
5.   This is a difficult time for her.
6.   She refuses to listen.
7.   She takes after her mother.
8.   I'm getting fed up with her.
9.   Her heart's in the right place.
10. She means well.
11. I'll do anything I can to help.
12. I've done everything I could to help.
13. I've lost hope.
14. She's got a lot of energy.
15. Girls will be girls.

5 Who is it?

Think of a very important person in your life. (It might be someone in your family, a friend, or even someone in your class.) Don't tell anyone who you are thinking of. Complete the following sentences about them. Then read your sentences to the rest of the class while they try to guess who you are talking about.

1. _____ _____ too much.

2. _____ refuses to _____

3. _____'s got a lot of _____ .

4. _____ is a bit on the _____ side.

5. _____ takes after his / her _____ .

6. This is a _____ time for _____ .

6 Discussion

What makes a good teacher? Number from 1 to 10 according to which you think is most important. Work in groups.

Makes the class fun	____
Uses many different kinds of material	____
Gives a lot of homework	____
Makes students work together	____
Explains everything	____
Talks a lot	____
Lets the class talk	____
Gives challenging tests	____
Is well prepared	____
Is flexible / Will change the lesson if necessary	____

What makes a good language student? Write the five most important things below.

1. _____

2. _____

3. _____

4. _____

5. _____

Is this a description of you? How could you become a better learner? What could you do more of? What could you do that you are not doing now?

DIFFICULT EXPLANATIONS

Silly Tatiana

Tatiana has had a very interesting experience. How well does she describe it? Complete this conversation using the sentences at the top of the next page.

Interviewer: So you say you've seen a UFO?

Tatiana: That's right.

Interviewer: And what happened exactly?

Tatiana: **(1)** _____

Interviewer: Well, why don't you start with what you saw first.

Tatiana: **(2)** _____

Interviewer: Did anyone come out?

Tatiana: Yes.

Interviewer: And what did they look like?

Tatiana: **(3)** _____

Interviewer: And did they speak to you?

Tatiana: **(4)** _____

Interviewer: I see. And what did they, er . . . say?

Tatiana: **(5)** _____

Interviewer: Souvenir?

Tatiana: **(6)** _____

Interviewer: And what did they want? Music? Some photographs?

Tatiana: **(7)** _____

Interviewer: Oh . . .

a. Well, for lack of a better word, like frogs. I can't think of any other way to describe them.
b. Something to the effect that they wanted something to bring home with them as a – what do you call it . . . .
c. Well, it's kind of hard to explain. Let's see. . . . how can I explain it . . . .
d. Right – something they could remember humans by.
e. California.
f. OK. Well, first there was this big ship – I don't know what else to call it . . . . and it landed right in front of my car.
g. Well, they didn't exactly speak, they . . . .What's the word I'm looking for? You know . . . . like when you can read someone's mind, or what have you.

1 Phrase Jumble

Ben is asking Gabi to marry him, but he's having trouble finding the right words. Put Ben's words in the correct order.

Ben:	1. Gabi, I think I _____?	*call what it do you.*
Gabi:	Love me, Ben?	
Ben:	2. Yeah, _____ .	*something that to effect*
Gabi:	Me too, Ben.	
Ben:	3. And maybe it's time for a _____?	*I'm what's looking the for word*
Gabi:	A commitment, Ben?	
Ben:	4. _____ .	*For better a of word lack*
Gabi:	And what would you like to do about it?	
Ben:	5. Sign a contract. . . . _____ .	*call what it else I know don't to*
Gabi:	A contract?	
Ben:	6. _____ .	*I other describe to way it any think can't of*
Gabi:	So you would like us to become, like, business partners?	
Ben:	7. _____ .	*Or couple a...have or what you*
Gabi:	But Ben, we're already a couple.	
Ben:	8. Yeah, but . . . . _____ .	*know you like real a couple*
Gabi:	A real couple?	
Ben:	9. _____ .	*It's hard kind explain to of*
Gabi:	I don't understand	
Ben:	10. _____?	*How it I explain can*
Gabi:	Are you asking me to marry you?	
Ben:	Yeah.	
Gabi:	No.	

Now go back and underline the important expressions. Then read the conversation in pairs so that it sounds as natural as possible. How many different ways can you say the last line?

2 Cloze

Which expression does _not_ complete the sentence correctly?

1. He said I wasn't very reliable, _____ .
   a. (or) something to that effect
   b. you know, like he didn't trust me
   c. I can't think of any other way to describe it

2. I thought it was just incredibly unfair, _____ .
   a. what do you call it...
   b. I can't think of any other way to describe it.
   c. I don't know what else to call it.

3. He's the manager _____, you know, the guy in charge.
   a. or what have you
   b. you know, like
   c. or something to that effect

4. Can you pass me the _____ . That thing over there.
   a. what do you call it?
   b. what's the word I'm looking for
   c. for lack of a better word

5. You want to know why we didn't call you? Well, _____ .
   a. or something to that effect
   b. it's kind of hard to explain
   c. how can I explain it

6. The sign said 'Trespassers will be prosecuted' or _____ .
   a. what have you
   b. something to that effect
   c. you know, like

7. A: So you think the reaction was, shall we say, hostile?
   a. B: Well, for lack of a better word, yes.
   b. B: What do you call it . . . .
   c. B: Well, I can't think of any other way to describe it.

8. She made this face. _____ when you have to sneeze.
   a. You know, like
   b. What do you call it
   c. It's kind of hard to explain

9. The driver of the other car was yelling _____ .
   a. what do you call it
   b. something to the effect that we were all to blame for the accident
   c. you know, like we were all to blame and he'd get fired

10. No. That's not what I mean. _____
    a. For lack of a better word . . . .
    b. How can I explain it. I mean . . . .
    c. It's kind of hard to explain . . . .

3 Dialogue Practice

1. Practice the dialogue in pairs.
2. Take turns being the Interviewer and Tatiana.
3. Practice until you can do the dialogue without reading it.
4. Do it for the class.

4 Expansion

Below are some of the words and phrases that English-speakers use when having problems explaining or describing something. Below, choose the phrase that is most similar to the phrase in boldface.

1. He talked about his life **and so on and so forth.**

   a. and many other things

   b. other things that I dare not mention

2. The food is **a little on the spicy side.**

   a. quite spicy

   b. not spicy enough

3. It's **greenish-blue.**

   a. half is green and half is blue

   b. between green and blue

4. It's very **human-like.**

   a. like a human

   b. pleasing to humans

5. The restaurant is very **arty.**

   a. full of paintings

   b. used by creative people

6. She's **sort of tall.**

   a. very tall

   b. more tall than short

7. It's **a cross between** an alsatian and a sheepdog.

   a. very much like both

   b. has qualities of both

8. I didn't eat it because there were **these insects** in it.

   a. the insects in my hand

   b. undefined / non-specified insects

9. He told me to give it to **some guy.**

   a. a man no one knows

   b. a man whose name is not important to me

10. She said that it would cost **such-and-such** amount.

    a. exact amount not important

    b. she never said the amount

11. And we said, "Hello", **blah, blah, blah.**

    a. you probably know the rest

    b. and no more

5 Storytelling

Now use the expressions you have learned and try to describe ONE of the following. Take five minutes to write down what you will say, and then tell it to a partner. Share it with the class.

1. Your first date (Who? Where? What did you do? What like? Conversation? Wearing?)
2. A game you played in your childhood (Who with? When? Where? Who taught you?)
3. A strange dream you've had (In color? When? Who? Clothes? Where?)
4. An exotic food you've tried (Taste? Ingredients? Restaurant? Cost?)
5. A song you like (The words? The message? What does the music sound like?)
6. Your hometown (The people? Their accent? Their clothes? What is the nightlife like?)

DESCRIBING THE IMPOSSIBLE

Grandpa Talltales

This unit will try to help you to say a lot, with just a little, in English. Johnny and his grandfather are fishing at a lake. Does Johnny believe his grandfather's story?

Johnny: Grandpa, Did you really see a Great White Shark when you were a sailor?

Grandpa: Did I? I could tell you stories.

Johnny: But were they big?

Grandpa: Just so you get an idea, I once mistook one of them for a ship.

Johnny: Were they bigger than Daddy's car?

Grandpa: Let's just say they could have eaten Daddy's car as an afternoon snack.

Johnny: But did you ever fight one?

Grandpa: If you only knew. I have had to go one-on-one with octopuses, man-eating sharks, and even pirates – just to name a few.

Johnny: Did a shark ever bite you?

Grandpa: Didn't I ever show you my left knee?

            [Grandpa lifts pant leg to show a scar]

Johnny: Wow! Did it hurt?

Grandpa: You could say that. That's nothing – you should see the one I have on my back.

Johnny: Is it really big, Grandpa?

Grandpa: Big? Let's put it this way: I don't know where my neck ends and that scar begins.

Johnny: Wow. Did a lot of people die, Grandpa?

Grandpa: Not many people survived, to put it mildly. Suffice it to say, I was one of the lucky ones.

Johnny: Wow, Grandpa. No one can tell totally unbelievable stories like you can.

1 Phrase Jumble

Re-write the following important expressions:

1. You could that say

   _____

2. If only knew you

   _____

3. I stories you tell could

   _____

4. Let's put it's this big it way

   _____

5. That's should my other you see nothing car

   _____

6. Suffice say it it's to cheap not

   _____

7. Let's just not say he's an Olympic athlete

   _____

8. It's mildly to it warm put out

   _____

9. I've name to few a China, Japan, and Singapore just been to

   _____

10. Just than idea learn get to you harder so an it's English

    _____

AND YOU CAN QUOTE ME ON THAT!

"The man who is too old to learn was probably always too old to learn."
Henry S. Haskins

Use five of the phrases above to respond in these situations:

11. Have you been in Asia?

    > _____

12. I love your red convertible!

    > _____

13. Your boyfriend looks like he needs a little exercise.

    > _____

14. Do I need to wear a jacket?

    > _____

15. I understand Tokyo is an expensive city.

    > _____

2 Wrong Use

Which phrase is natural and which is not in these pairs:

1. a. He's not exactly handsome, let's put it that way.
   b: He's not exactly handsome, let's put it this way.

2. a. Smart? Let's just say she is intelligent.
   b. Smart? Let's just say she makes Einstein seem dumb.

3. a. He is so, so old – to put it mildly.
   b. He's not young anymore – to put it mildly.

4. a. Just so you get an idea, here's my car.
   b. Just so you get an idea, here's a picture of my car.

5. a. They have dogs, cats and fish – just to name a few.
   b. They have several pets – just to name a few.

6. a. You work too hard. If you only knew.
   b. Do they work too hard? If you only knew.

7. a. That's nothing – you should see my other one.
   b. That's nothing – you'd better see my other one.

8. a. Was she strong? I could tell you stories.
   b. They say she's strong. I could tell you stories.

3 Dialogue Practice

1. Practice the dialogue in pairs.
2. Take turns being Johnny and Grandpa.
3. Practice until you can do the dialogue without reading it.
4. Do it for the class.

4 Complete the Sentence

Complete the following with your own personal information. Then work in pairs. Take turns asking questions to get these responses:

1. Am I good looking? Let's just say _____ .

2. I'm multi-talented. I can _____ , and _____ , and _____
   – just to name a few.

3. Suffice it to say my English is _____ .

4. Am I _____ ? If you only knew!

5. I _____ money, to put it mildly.

6. Is that your salary? That's nothing, _____ .

7. Am I intelligent? Lets put it this way . . . . _____ .

8. Famous? Just so you get an idea, the other day, _____ .

9. _____ ? You could say that.

10. Do I _____ ? I could tell you stories.

5 Role Play – Bragging about your Hometown

Write five things that make your town special. Then find a partner whose hometown is not the same as yours. Using phrases from this unit, tell your partner whose town is better. Share the debate with the class. Whose town is really the best?

My hometown is _____. Five things which make it special are:

1. _____
2. _____
3. _____
4. _____
5. _____

6 Discussion

Below is a survey taken from World Traveler Magazine. Do you agree? Which would you add?

10 Most Romantic Cities

1. Paris, France
2. Düsseldorf, Germany
3. Venice, Italy
4. San Francisco, USA
5. Kyoto, Japan
6. Tai Pei, Taiwan
7. Buenos Aires, Argentina
8. London, England
9. Seoul, Korea
10. Casablanca, Morocco

10 Best Kinds of Food

1. Mexican
2. Italian
3. Catalan
4. American (USA)
5. Chinese
6. Thai
7. Swiss
8. English
9. Indian
10. French

10 Most Polite Nationalities

1. Americans (USA)
2. Japanese
3. British
4. Persians
5. French
6. Greek
7. Salvadorans
8. Brazilians
9. Koreans
10. Canadians

10 Best Year-Round Climate

1. Quito, Ecuador
2. Miami, USA
3. Rome, Italy
4. Seattle, USA
5. San Juan, Puerto Rico
6. Valencia, Spain
7. Cairo, Egypt
8. Kinshasa, Zaire
9. Dakar, Senegal
10. San Antonio, USA

CONVERSATION FRAME 2

Enthusiastic Mario

One of the hardest things to do for someone who is learning another language is to express different kinds of emotion – especially strong or excited emotion. What pattern do you see in what Mario says?

Elizabeth: How did you like the play?

Mario: Great. I've seen some great performances before, but Phantom of the Opera has to be the greatest.

Elizabeth: What about the music? Not bad, eh?

Mario: I'll say. I've heard some good music before, but that music has to be the best.

1 Pattern Practice

So the pattern is:

I've _seen_ some _bad performances_ before, but _that_ has to be the _worst._

| verb | adjective + noun | noun / pronoun | superlative adjective |

Work in pairs to complete the following:

1. I've _____ some spicy food before, but _____ has to be the _____ .

2. I've _____ some _____ before, but San Francisco has to be the _____ .

3. I've _____ some _____ before, but The Louvre has to be the _____ .

4. I've _____ some _____ before, but English has to be the _____ .

5. I've _____ some long books before, but _____ has to be the _____ .

6. I've _____ some _____ films before, but _____ has to be the _____ .

7. I've _____ some _____ bad days before, but _____ has to be the _____ .

8. I've _____ some brilliant TV shows before, but _____ has to be the _____ .

Now do the same with the following:

9. bad vacations

10. stupid jokes

11. lousy roommates

12. bad dreams

13. brilliant ideas

14. great actors

15. delicious steaks

16. hot summers

41

2 Insults

Use the frame you just practiced to answer these question with an insult. For example:

Do you like my nose?
> No. I've seen some big noses before, but yours has to be the biggest.

1. How do you like my house?

2. How do you like my husband?

3. What do you think about my English?

4. How do you like my new hairdo?

5. How do you like my new car?

6. Did you enjoy the dessert I made?

7. Do you like the wine I've chosen?

8. So how do you like London?

9. Have you enjoyed our date?

10. Did you like my joke?

3 Superlatives

Without consulting with a fellow student, fill in the most obvious superlative adjective in the following expressions. Then fill in the right-hand column on your own.

1. the _____ river in America   *The Mississipi* _____

2. the _____ river in the world   _____

3. the _____ city in America   _____

4. the _____ city in the world   _____

5. the _____ company in America   _____

6. the _____ multinational company in the world   _____

7. the _____ popular of the British royals   _____

8. the _____ popular of the British royals   _____

9. the _____ invention the world has seen   _____

10. the _____ drug in the world   _____

11. the _____ problem facing the world today   _____

12. the _____ mistake I have ever made   _____

Compare your answers with a partner and then with the whole class. Did you agree?

4 More Insults

Using things around you, make insults with your partner – only for fun! Use the frame.
For example:

I've sat in some uncomfortable desks before, but these have to be the most.
I've eaten some lousy burgers before, but this has to be the worst.

5 Discuss – Who's the best?

Below, discuss who / which is the best.

1. Which country makes the most delicious food?

2. Who makes the nicest car?

3. Which country makes the finest wine?

4. Who is the best boxer of all time?

5. Which is the most romantic city in the world?

6. Who is the best writer of all time?

7. Which country makes the best cheese in the world?

8. Which nationality are the best language learners in the world?

Now in your class try to discover who is the best swimmer / singer / dancer / cook? Who is the most generous, the most interesting, the most charming student?
Try to discover your own superlative people!

TELLING A STORY

A New Item on the Menu

In English, you can probably already tell something about what you do, what your hobbies are, and where you are from. You can probably even tell a story, but what about if you want the listener to feel excited about what you are saying? Natalie, a restaurant manager, is telling her friend about a difficult day at work. Would you eat at her restaurant? Use the sentences at the top of the next page to complete this conversation.

Natalie: **(1)** _____

Jimmy: What.

Natalie: **(2)** _____

Jimmy: A cockroach? Is that all?

Natalie: **(3)** _____

Jimmy: How big was it?

Natalie: **(4)** _____

Jimmy: So what did you do?

Natalie: **(5)** _____

Jimmy: Were they angry?

Natalie: **(6)** _____

Jimmy: That's not very good, is it?

Natalie: **(7)** _____

Jimmy: So what did you end up doing with the roach?

Natalie: **(8)** _____

a. Yeah, but this was not your average cockroach. You should've seen this thing. I mean, talk about ugly. Not only that – it was huge.

b. Angry? We're talking downright furious! Not only did they scream and yell at me, but they called the health inspector.

c. I'm cleaning a table, right, when all of a sudden everyone starts pointing to the floor and screaming "Cockroach! Cockroach!"

d. Big. I'm telling you, this thing was so big that I thought it was a dog at first. I mean, I literally thought it was a dog.

e. You wouldn't believe what happened today at the restaurant.

f. Well, let's put it this way: Don't eat the chicken special tomorrow.

g. Not at all. I mean, it was so bad that I literally had to call the police to keep them from getting violent.

h. It's not what I did . . . . it's what the customers did. You want to talk about complaints . . . .

1 What's the Phrase?

Using the cues, complete these two sets of sentences.

1. But this was not your	a. downright furious!
2. You should've	b. ugly!
3. I mean, talk about	c. seen this thing – it was huge!
4. We're talking	d. but they called the health inspector.
5. Not only did they scream and yell at me,	e. average cockroach.
6. I was cleaning, when all of a	f. believe what happened to me today!
7. I'm telling	g. that I thought it was a dog.
8. This thing was so big	h. you, they were angry.
9. You wouldn't	i. about complaints . . . .
10. You want to talk	j. sudden everyone starts pointing at the floor and screaming.

Now go back and underline the important phrases. For example: _not your average_.

2 Pattern Practice

With a partner, fill in the boxes below with your own examples. Your teacher will help.

1. He was so		that	
2. You wouldn't believe	what how the way		
3. Not only does she		but	
4. I was		when all of a sudden	

3 Dialogue Practice

1. Practice the dialogue in pairs.
2. Take turns being Jimmy and Natalie.
3. Practice until you can do the dialogue without reading it.
4. Do it for the class.

4 Gap Fill

Complete the short story with the phrases below:

talk about	*should've seen*	*I'm telling you*
we're talking	*was not your average*	

I once had a chance to make a lot of money – 1. _____ a lot.
But 2. _____ bad luck – my dog had eaten my lottery ticket!
And, 3. _____, this 4. _____ jackpot. It was at
least $25 million! You 5. _____ my husband's face when I
told him what happened. That is, my ex-husband.

5 Expansion – *I mean, literally,* and *this*

You probably noticed that I *mean*, *literally* and *this* were words repeated in the dialogue. These words also help to give emphasis when telling stories. Use them in the sentences below:

1. He has a lot of money – _____ a lot.

2. You should've seen the money he had.

   _____ guy was rich.

3. _____ , talk about angry.

4. We _____ had to steal our

   food in order to eat.

5. _____ place was huge!

6. _____ , _____

   dog _____ ate my homework!

7. I'm telling you, we were starving. _____ ,

   _____ starving.

8. _____ , you couldn't cut

   _____ steak if your life depended on it.

I MEAN, THIS DOG *LITERALLY* ATE MY HOMEWORK!

Today's Lesson:

6 Role Play – The one that got away

Be one of the following:

a. A police officer
b. A hunter
c. A fisherman
d. A newspaper reporter

Talk about:

A tough criminal
Bigfoot
A great white shark
A big story

You will tell an incredible story based on your profession. The story should include phrases from the dialogue and exercises. You may take five minutes to write what you will say, and then share it with your partner – then tell the class.
Here is an example to help you.

> **A newspaper reporter:** You wouldn't believe the story I almost got one day. I was walking to my car, when all of a sudden I saw these two guys robbing a bank. You should've seen how many guns they had – talk about heavily armed. Not only that – they had taken three hostages! I'm telling you, I was scared. But you want to talk about bad luck . . . . I didn't have my camera! I mean, I literally had forgotten my camera. So then . . . ."

7 Discussion

The following piece of an advice column appeared recently in a newspaper:

> Dear Abby,
> The things that happen to me in normal life aren't really exciting. So when I'm at a party and people are telling all kinds of funny and exciting stories, sometimes I find a story that is a little interesting and I change it a little to make it very interesting. That's not lying is it? I mean, what would you do? Am I the only one who does this?
> Lucille

How would you answer Lucille's last three questions?

BEING POLITE

Proud Wilbur

Armando and Angelina are visiting a family who have just moved in upstairs. Do they regret their visit?

Wilbur:	And did I tell you that Richard won first prize in the school poetry contest?
Armando:	How about that.
Angelina:	(*under her breath*) Big deal.
Wilbur:	Oh . . . and did I show you his football trophy? (*takes it off the shelf*)
Armando:	Isn't that something.
Angelina:	(*to Armando*) So what?
Wilbur:	He's so sweet. You know, he brings us breakfast every morning.
Armando:	Can't beat that.
Angelina:	(*smiles bitterly*)
Wilbur:	Oh, you must see the ash tray he made for us. Is he artistic, or what?
Armando:	I must admit, he does show some talent.
Angelina:	(*to herself*) I've seen better.
Armando:	(*looking around*) Hey, Wilbur. Who decorated your place?
Wilbur:	Giovanna, my wife. She did it herself – isn't that something?
Angelina:	Quite impressive.
Armando:	(*to himself*) Big deal.
Wilbur:	And she made that beautiful chair you're sitting on. Not bad, eh?
Angelina:	Looks like a lot of work, I must admit.
Armando:	It's OK, I guess.

1 Matching

In pairs, make a phrase by matching the correct word(s). Try to do it without the dialogue.

1. I must	_____	a. or what?
2. Quite	_____	b. something?
3. How about	_____	c. that.
4. So	_____	d. that.
5. Not	_____	e. OK.
6. Is he artistic	_____	f. what?
7. Big	_____	g. better.
8. I've seen	_____	h. impressive.
9. Isn't that	_____	i. admit, he does play the piano well.
10. It's	_____	j. deal.
11. Can't beat	_____	k. bad, eh?

2 Sorting

Sort the phrases above into the three boxes below. Some may be used more than once. Compare with a partner.

Meaning: Aren't you impressed?

_____
_____
_____
_____

Meaning: I'm impressed.

_____
_____
_____
_____

Meaning: I'm not impressed.

_____
_____
_____
_____

3 Pair Work

1. **What other verbs could substitute _seen_ in I've _seen better_, if you were responding to the following statements:**

a. This chicken's delicious.	> I've _____ better!
b. This is one of the best cups of coffee I've ever had.	> I've _____ better!
c. Your car sure is fast, and it handles great.	> I've _____ better!
d. I really like that CD. They're a really nice group.	> I've _____ better!
e. Not a bad book, eh?	> I've _____ better!
f. Does this airline have good service, or what?	> I've _____ better!

2. **What other words can substitute _something_ in _isn't that something_? Give examples.**

3. **Not _bad_ and Not _bad, eh_? mean the same thing. True of False?**

4. **How _about this_ and How _about that_ mean the same thing. True or False?**

5. **Another way of saying So _what_? is And _what_? True or False?**

6. **Possible or Impossible?**
    - A: "Is he fast, or what?"
    - B: a. Sure is.
      - b. I'll say.
      - c. He's quick, I must admit.
      - d. It's OK.

7. **Possible or Impossible?**
    - A: "Isn't he talented?"
    - B: a. Big deal.
      - b. It's a deal.
      - c. It's really no big deal.

8. **How can the way you say It's OK change the meaning?**

4 Dialogue Practice

Work in groups of three playing Wilbur, Angelina, and Armando. Try the following sequence:

1. Read the dialogue sitting down.
2. Read it while physically acting out the scene.
3. Do it without the script as much as possible, until you feel comfortable.
4. Do it for the class.

5 Discussion

1. What does the word 'vanity' mean? Are you vain? When passing a shop, do you look at your own reflection in the glass? Do you know someone who is vain? What do they do?
2. Armando and Angelina both get a little jealous. Do you get jealous easily? When was the last time you were jealous of someone? What would make you jealous? Do you let people know you are jealous? How do you react?

6 Role Play – Your Dream Home

Play the following characters. Use phrases from the dialogue.

Husband	You want to but a new home, and quickly.
Wife	You are happy where you are. You don't want a new home.
Real Estate Agent	You need to sell one of the homes (see advertisement).

Be sure to spend 10 minutes preparing what you will say as a group, then after practicing, let the class watch.

20+ SOLD IN 30

NEW CITY HOMES.
NEW NEIGHBORHOOD.
FROM $99,000.

WIDE SELECTION

Come pick out a new San Francisco condominium home located right in the City's most convenient neighborhood.

PRICING

Studios from $99,000 – just $999 a month!
1-bedrooms from $169,000
2-bedrooms from $189,000

FINE LIVING FEATURES

* Ten-minute walk to Financial District
* Enclosed parking and 24-hour doorman
* Heated pool
* Fitness Center
* Sauna
* At the heart of restaurant row and the liveliest nightlife in town
* Easy financing

RM Properties

LESSON 12

CONVERSATION TABOOS 2

Dance Class

It is important to know how to be tactful when telling someone that they've got something wrong. Some people are very proud and take offense easily if they are not corrected in a delicate manner. Something is not right with this conversation. With a partner, decide what should be changed.

Instructor: OK. So, it's one-two-three, one-two-three. Got it?

Student: (*student tries*) Like this?

Instructor: That's completely wrong.

Student: (*tries again*) How about now?

Instructor: Only a little better. Watch again. (*shows student again*)

Student: (*student tries*) Like this?

Instructor: Wrong. You'll never get it.

Student: Well, maybe if I practice enough I can dance like Fred Astaire.

Instructor: Don't make me laugh.

With a partner, re-write the conversation. The phrases below will help you.

I think you're on the right track	*not exactly*
Well, I don't know about **that**	*I wouldn't go* **that** *far*
you'll get the hang of it	*you've got the right idea*

When you finish:

1. Ask the teacher for more suggestions
2. Practice the new conversation with and then without script
3. Act out the new conversation , then show the class

1 Role Play

> A: *Wow! S/he's a great dancer. I'm going to ask her/him to dance.*
>
> B: *Sorry. I saw her/him first.*

In pairs, decide:

1. Who is A?

2. Who is B?

3. Where are they? (i.e. A disco? What kind of disco?)

4. Make a complete conversation until you reach a solution.

5. Your teacher will ask you to show the class.

2 What would you say?

Your boss has just told you something that you know is wrong and idiotic. Which of the following would you find appropriate to say?

1. That's an interesting way of looking at it.

2. I've never thought of it that way before.

3. You're joking, right?

4. You think so?

5. Are you sure about that?

6. I understand what you're saying.

7. What are you talking about?

8. Are you serious?

9. I don't see it that way.

10. You're wrong.

11. I'll have to think about it some more.

12. Maybe.

13. Is that what you think?

14. What makes you say that?

15. Well . . . . I don't know.

Which ones would be sure to get you dismissed?

3 Discussion

1. Do you consider yourself a perfectionist?
2. Do you give up easily?
3. Do you prefer to do only those things which you do well?
4. If someone corrects your English, do you feel embarrassed?

LESSON 13

REACTING PREDICTABLY
Stuart Gets Sacked

Getting negative information and then reacting to it in a natural way – that is what this unit is about. Complete the conversation using the phrases at the top of the next page. There is only one correct order. Stuart is talking with his co-worker. Why does he lose his job?

Stuart:	(1)	_____
Mayumi:	Jeff – Who else?	
Stuart:	(2)	_____
Mayumi:	It never fails. It's not what you know, but *who* you know.	
Stuart:	(3)	_____
Mayumi:	It looks like the boss didn't even consider us.	
Stuart:	(4)	_____
Mayumi:	More than you.	
Stuart:	(5)	_____
Mayumi:	Of course.	
Stuart:	(6)	_____
Mayumi:	The boss promoted her, too.	
Stuart:	(7)	_____
Mayumi:	Yours.	
Stuart:	(8)	_____

a. As usual. And how much are they going to pay him?

b. So . . . Who got the promotion?

c. I was afraid of that.

d. Figures – the boss' nephew. I should've known.

e. I had a feeling he would. So what job does she have now?

f. I thought so. And Jeff's sister, Dee?

g. Just as I thought. And I'll bet he got a company car.

h. Typical. Everyone said he was going to get it, and sure enough . . .

1 Phrase Correction

Each phrase below has something that makes it wrong (for this unit). Circle the mistakes and check with a partner.

1. Topical.
2. I think so.
3. Like usual.
4. It's figured.
5. As I thought.
6. It seldom fails.
7. I must've known.
8. I was scared of that.
9. Jeff – who otherwise?
10. I had a sensation he would.
11. I'd bet he got a company car.
12. It's sure enough, he got the promotion.

2 Gap Fill

Now put in a correct phrase from the exercise above to complete the sentences below.

1. Chicken again? ._____ known.

2. _____ you were going to call me.

3. He ran off with his secretary. _____ .

4. Who perfected that technology? The Germans, _____?

5. _____ fails – you jump in the shower and the phone rings.

6. _____ you don't really speak Japanese, do you?

7. Sold out?_____ .

8. _____ you're the manager because you're the only one wearing a tie.

9. It _____ . I made my lunch this morning but forgot to bring it.

10. On time, _____ Mr. Hill.

11. _____ enough – my keys were in my jacket.

12. So you were the one who took my umbrella. _____ so.

Now go back and underline all the phrases used in this lesson to respond to negative information.

3 Joke Match

Choose a line from the box below to complete the following jokes:

> *a. I had a feeling you were coming!*
> *b. From Daddy – who else?*
> *c. I was afraid of that.*
> *d. I'll bet that's for me!*
> *e. But honey, we have been for 30 years!*
> *f. But we're at the restaurant!*
> *g. Dog? That's my husband!*
> *h. But mommy – that's mine!*
> *i. But doesn't she wear contacts?*
> *j. It figures that you wouldn't remember me.*
> *k. Really? I can't even imagine what the life of a long-distance operator is like.*

1. A: As usual your dog seems to be in perfect health, Mrs. Baker
   B: _____

2. A: Just as I thought! You're married!
   B: _____

3. A: What did the psychic say when the guests arrived?
   B: _____

4. A: What did the prisoner say when the phone in his cell rang?
   B: _____

5. A: It never fails. You tell the maid to be careful and she still shrinks your favorite sweater!
   B: _____

6. A: And do you take John to be your lawfully wedded husband?
   B: I do.
   C: _____

7. A: Knock knock
   B: Who's there?
   A: Figgers.
   B: Figgers who?
   A: _____

8. A: Where did you hear such a filthy word, young man!
   B: _____

9. A: How typical! The men aren't lifting a finger to wash the dishes.
   B: _____

10. A: I should've known she liked my husband. She was always winking at him.
    B: _____

11. A: Back in school, we knew Wendy's voice would be heard all around the world, and sure enough . . .
    B: _____

4 Dialogue Practice

1. Practice the dialogue in pairs.
2. Take turns being Stuart and Mayumi.
3. Practice until you can do the dialogue without reading it.
4. Do it for the class.

5 Who said it?

Mr. Jones and Mrs. Jones are a happily married suburban couple who have two children – one boy, and one girl. Below are some things they have said recently – but not necessarily to each other. Can you guess who said what? Work with a partner.

1. It's my car, too.
2. Dinner's ready!
3. What's for dinner?
4. How's my hair?
5. Where did I put the remote control?
6. I've fallen in love with someone else.
7. Will you marry me?
8. Isn't she cuuute!
9. Would you like me to walk you to your car?
10. Can you open this for me?
11. I'm getting married!
12. I'm getting wrinkles.
13. Can I give you a hand, honey?
14. Have you seen my shoes? I can't find them.
15. How do I look?
16. Do we *have* to go to your mother's for dinner?
17. I don't want to always have to clean up your mess.
18. You left the toilet seat up.
19. Oh! It's simply beautiful!
20. Let me help you with your coat.
21. You're cute when you're angry.
22. Yesterday was our wedding anniversary. You forgot.
23. Not tonight. . . I have a headache.
24. Are you listening to me?

6 Role Play

Work in pairs. Study the following instructions:

Student A
Look at the headlines below. Pretend you're reading a newspaper and mention them to B.
For example:

The headline says:	*President says he'll raise taxes.*
You say to B:	*Looks like the President's going to raise taxes again.*
Useful phrases for A:	*Looks like . . . . Says here that . . . . Listen to this . . . .*

Student B
Keep your book closed. React to the headlines using phrases from the dialogue. Take turns being A.
For example: *Figures.*

Unemployment at all-time high	Bruce Willis to star in new action film
Bad weather predicted for weekend	Crime rate up for third year in a row
Scandal in the Royal Family	Joan Collins to marry again
Cost of education soars to new high	New study shows restaurant-dining harmful
English most widely-spoken language, says expert	Americans unsatisfied with Parisian service
French unsatisfied with English food	Queen actually a man!
Japanese score higher on tests than Americans	Men get higher pay, better jobs
Devastating forest fire caused by cigarette	Most American Olympic athletes took steroids
UFO sighting a fake	Economists see no end to inflation
McDonald's to build first restaurant on moon	Housing prices up thirty per cent
Lunatic threatens to kill Mayor, says he heard 'voices'	Seismologist: Earthquake 'likely' in California within the next 30 years

COMFORTING

Maryanne the Musician

Maryanne, Michael's co-worker, is crying. What does Michael try to do? Is he successful?

Michael:	Maryanne . . . . What's the matter?
Maryanne:	The producer only laughed at me this time.
Michael:	Oh, don't let it get to you, Maryanne. Before you know it people will begin to appreciate 'disco-polka'.
Maryanne:	Yeah, maybe. It's just that I never seem to succeed.
Michael:	Don't worry about it. If it makes you feel any better, it took eight years before anyone noticed my paintings.
Maryanne:	I don't think I'll ever get another chance.
Michael:	Look, if worst comes to worst you can always go back to school. It's really no big deal.
Maryanne:	Yeah, I suppose.
Michael:	Hey, look at it this way – at least you're not teaching English anymore. And who knows, maybe one day you *will* get discovered.
Maryanne:	You're probably right. Maybe I'll get lucky next time.
Michael:	You never know. Things always have a way of working themselves out.
Maryanne:	Thanks, Michael. Hey . . . . Would you like to listen to my new song?
Michael:	Actually, I think I have to go home and make dinner soon. Thanks anyway.
Maryanne:	Figures.

1 Matching

In pairs, make a phrase by matching the beginnings with the endings in the box below:
Try to do it without the dialogue.

1. If worst comes _____
2. It's no big _____
3. Look at it _____
4. Who _____
5. You never _____
6. Don't worry _____
7. You'll find a job before you _____
8. If it makes you _____
9. Don't let it _____
10. Things always have a way _____

---

a. this way: you still have your health.
b. know.
c. deal.
d. of working themselves out.
e. to worst we can ask for a loan.
f. get to you.
g. feel any better, I failed that test twice.
h. about it.
i. knows – maybe she'll call you back.
j. know it.

Some phrases are 'whole' phrases because they can be used alone without more words.
Mark these with a 'w'. Compare with a partner.
Now go back. One person read the beginning of the phrase and let your partner fill in the blank without looking.

2 Pairwork

Using the phrases above (two have similar meanings), what's another way of saying:

1. This problem is not as important as you think it is.
2. I'll tell you something that has happened to me which is even worse than your problem.
3. You can forget about this problem because it will be solved with or without you.
4. Even if the problem does not improve, everything will be fine.
5. You can interpret this problem in a more optimistic way.
6. Things will get better very, very soon.
7. It's possible (but not likely) something good could happen.
8. It's better not to think about it too much.
9. Don't take this problem so personally.

3 Dialogue Practice

1. Practice the dialogue in pairs.
2. Take turns being Michael and Maryanne.
3. Practice until you can do the dialogue without reading it.
4. Do it for the class.

4 Dialogue Building

Working in pairs, make a dialogue. One person will comfort the other. Write the dialogue on a piece of paper, passing the paper back and forth – each one writing a new line. All phrases should be used. The dialogue must begin with one of the following:

I got another speeding ticket!

I didn't get accepted at the university.

My English never seems to get any better.

My hair is getting grey.

Our client in London changed her mind at the last minute.

The boss gave the promotion to some kid half my age.

S/he said s/he doesn't love me anymore.

Now read the dialogue for the class.

5 Worries 1

Below are some worries different people have expressed. First, find which ones are:

a. A friend learning to dance
b. A friend trying to lose weight
c. A friend discouraged about their cooking
d. A grandmother thinking about a new career.

Then, write five more worries these people might express under each one.

1. _____
Nothing seems to work.
I'm afraid to get on the scale.
I can't even go to the beach.
I might as well give up.
I'm tired of dieting.
_____
_____
_____
_____
_____

2. _____
I have two left feet.
I have no sense of rhythm.
Everyone else is better than me.
I look stupid.
I think people are staring at me.
_____
_____
_____
_____
_____

3. _____

I'm too old.
I don't have any time to study.
Everyone will think I'm the teacher.
I haven't studied in years.
I'm not a teenager any more.

_____

_____

_____

_____

_____

4. _____

It burned again!.
I don't do anything right.
My chicken tastes like wood.
I'll just eat out.
People never ask for seconds.

_____

_____

_____

_____

_____

6 Worries 2

Working with a partner, read out the worries from exercise 5, and your partner will try to comfort you using the language learned in this unit.

7 Discussion

1. **Do you use these phrases – or similar ones – in your language?**

2. **When you have a problem, Do you prefer to be left alone or be comforted?**
   Why or Why not?

3. **What would you say to:**

   1. A friend whose cat died

   2. A friend whose father is in the hospital

   3. A friend who has lost her job

   4. A friend who is having marriage problems

   5. A son / daughter who has failed university exams

   6. A friend whose car was vandalized

   7. A friend whose promotion fell through

   8. A spouse who is trying to lose weight

   9. A spouse who thinks (s)he can't cook

   10. A boss who is worried about the future of the company

CONVERSATION FRAME 3

Not a Nice Daddy

This lesson helps you use a frame for explaining why you don't agree. It helps you to find something right in what someone else might think is wrong, and to find something wrong in what someone else might think is right.

Junior:	Daddy, I'm tired.
Daddy:	Tired? I mean, I could see if you worked all day or something, but you just watch TV.
Junior:	But I'm also hungry.
Daddy:	Hungry? I mean, I could see if you hadn't eaten in over a year or something, but you ate just last week.
Junior:	Daddy, will you buy me a bar of chocolate?
Daddy:	A bar of chocolate? I mean, I could see if we were rich or something, but we barely have enough money to pay for the new Ferrari. Sorry.

1 Pattern Practice

Now make more sentences like Daddy's. Work in pairs. For example:

A: You're under arrest.

B: *Under arrest? I mean, I could see if I had murdered somebody or something, but I only stole a couple of police cars, officer.*

1. A: You're fired!
   B: _____

2. A: I want a divorce.
   B: _____

3. A: You need to lose weight.
   B: _____

4. A: You must stop driving so fast.
   B: _____

5. A: If you don't study more you'll fail the test.
   B: _____

6. A: Could you turn on the heat?
   B: _____

7. A: Shouldn't you cut down on smoking a bit?
   B: _____

8. A: Are you going to be long? I need to use the phone.
   B: _____

9. A: I think you've had a little too much to drink.
   B: _____

10. A: You should say you're sorry to that little boy.
    B: _____

2 Pair Work

Now your partner will talk about problems that s/he finds in the items below, and you will answer them using the frame. Take turns. For example:

A: *This room is too small.*

B: *Too small? I mean, I could see if (we had fifty people in this class, but there's only you and me!)*

1. the classroom
2. your accent
3. the town where you are now
4. your car

5. the environment
6. the weather
7. the amount of money you earn
8. your hair

3 Discussion – Moving Violations

Below are some items that are considered traffic violations. Put the problems in order of seriousness with your partner. Compare the results with the class.

no signal	*burned-out headlight*	*illegal turn*
driving under the influence	*speeding*	*double-parking*
parking in a handicapped zone	*expired parking meter*	*driving without a license*
driving without a license plate	*baby not in infant-seat*	*passing on the right*
not coming to a complete stop at a stop sign		
driving while not wearing a seatbelt		

Do you have the same traffic laws in your country? Any ones not mentioned here? Some countries have different traffic laws about the following:

using a mobile phone while driving
using seatbelts in town v. seatbelts out of town
no alcohol v. a little alcohol
fines v. imprisonment

4 Mr. Belittle

Write down at least five things you are proud of in your life. They should be true, but do not have to be:

1. _____
2. _____
3. _____
4. _____
5. _____

Work with a partner. Try to belittle each other's points – just for fun! For example:

A: *I once saw Dustin Hoffman in a supermarket.*
B: *Big deal! I mean, I could see if you had dinner with him or something, but just to see him . . . . .*

After practicing with a partner, try doing the same activity with the class.
Fill in the box below with comments from your classmates

I mean, I could see if   or something, but

5 The Ideal Parent

The parent in the dialogue was not the ideal. What qualities does the ideal parent have? From the following eight areas, choose one sentence which describes the kind of parent you would like to be:

1. BABY CRYING

a. I would let the baby cry. Parents who run everytime they hear a cry are only asking for trouble later on.

b. If the baby is crying, it needs comfort. I would go immediately and do my best to find out why it was crying.

2. CANDIES

a. I don't allow them in the house. I lost all my teeth by the time I was 20 – all because of too much candy.

b. Ban candy and they'll get it from their friends. I don't ban anything.

3. HOMEWORK

a. My kids know that they don't get fed till they've done their homework.

b. It's up to them. If they don't do it, their teacher is mad with them. That's the best lesson for life. Let them make their own mistakes – that's my philosophy.

4. THE LATEST COMPUTER GAME

a. I feel that if my kids don't have the same as everyone else in their class, they will grow up feeling deprived – just like I did. No child of mine will ever feel deprived.

b. Too many parents give in to every demand their kids make. I don't. They get $30 a week pocket money and when that is finished, they don't get one cent more.

5. VACATION

a. My parents took me camping every summer and that's what I intend doing with my kids – fresh air and the open road – what more does a kid want?

b. My kids are going to see the world. I can't wait to take them to Paris, Rome, Sydney – all the places I wanted to go when I was young.

6. ALCOHOL

a. No child of mine will taste alcohol in my house – ever.

b. I'm going to educate my kids to drink – just like they do in France. First a drop of wine with water, then when they're older, they will keep alcohol in its place – unlike kids who grew up with prohibition at home.

7. SEX

a. I'm a child of the sixties. It was a great time.

b. No sex before marriage. It's as simple as that.

8. POLITICS

a. I would never try to impose my politics on any child of mine. They will grow up and make up their own minds.

b. My father and his father before him were Republicans. I would do my best to make sure my kids followed in the family tradition.

SHARING SECRETS

Insider Information

Somewhere in Spain, around 1490. Margarita is a chambermaid in Queen Isabelle's castle. She's talking to her friend, Elias, at the local market. Who is the visitor they're talking about? The missing lines are at the top of the next page.

Elias:	I hate being a fisherman. There must be an easier way to make money.
Margarita:	**(1)** _____
Elias:	Sure.
Margarita:	**(2)** _____
Elias:	OK, OK. So, How can I make easy money?
Margarita:	**(3)** _____
Elias:	What do you mean 'round' maps?
Margarita:	**(4)** _____
Elias:	So? Who will believe him, anyway?
Margarita:	**(5)** _____
Elias:	What makes you think that?
Margarita:	**(6)** _____
Elias:	Wow . . . even the Queen believes him. So if the world is really round, then maps will also have to be round. I'll be a millionaire!
Margarita:	**(7)** _____
Elias:	Don't worry, your secret's safe with me. Anyway . . . . Who would believe me?

a. Well, I don't want this to get around, but the Queen is giving him some ships, and off the record, a lot of money.

b. Round . . . . like a ball. Look, I'll let you in on a little secret: There's a man here from Genoa – I won't mention any names – and he thinks the world is round.

c. Maybe I can help you. Can you keep a secret?

d. (*whispering*) You didn't hear this from me – if word gets out that I'm giving away Royal secrets they'll fire me for sure.

e. Well, just between you and me, I think he might prove it.

f. Exactly. Now, I don't want the whole world to know so don't tell anyone. OK?

g. Start a round map business.

1 Matching

In pairs, make a phrase by matching the correct word(s). Try to do it without the dialogue.

1. I'll let you in	a. gets out that I'm single again . . . . look out.
2. Off the	b. get around.
3. Can you keep a	c. on a little secret: the diamond is fake.
4. I won't mention	d. from me, but I think she likes you.
5. You didn't hear this	e. record, I think you should get the promotion.
6. Just between	f. world to know.
7. If word	g. secret?
8. Your secret's	h. any names.
9. I don't want the whole	i. you and me, his cooking is disgusting!
10. I don't want this to	j. safe with me.

2 Practice

Mark has just told his friend Terrence that he wants to marry his sister. Read what Terrence says and with a partner fill in the blanks with an expression from above.

So . . . . you want to marry my sister, do you? Don't worry, your secret's 1. _____ .Can you keep 2. _____? Now, you didn't hear this 3. _____, but I think my sister has a thing for you, too. You want to know how to win her heart? I'll let you in on 4. _____ – she loves chocolates. Now, I don't want this to get 5. _____, but I know another young man, I won't mention 6. _____, who is also interested in my sister, but, just between 7. _____, I think he's no good for her. Now, off the 8._____, since I like you, and also because you drive that nice new red convertible that only a guy as nice as you would let me borrow, I'm going to do my best to say only good things about you to my sister. Remember, though, I don't want the whole 9. _____, because if word 10. _____ that I'm helping you, my sister will kill me.

Now go back and underline the phrases for using discretion. When you have done that, work with a partner. Take turns reading what Terrence said out loud. Pause where there is a space and let your partner complete the expression.

3 Cloze

In pairs, choose a phrase to complete the sentence.

1. And the person who is responsible, _____, is no longer with R & A, Ltd.
   - a. I won't mention any names
   - b. you didn't hear this from me
   - c. your secret's safe with me
   - d. I don't want the whole world to know

2. Well, I think Josie's lying – _____ .
   - a. just between you and me
   - b. I won't mention any names
   - c. I'll let you in on a little secret
   - d. your secret's safe with me

3. _____ – I'm getting married!
   - a. You didn't hear this from me
   - b. Your secret's safe with me
   - c. Can you keep a secret?
   - d. If word gets out that

4. _____ – we're not really married.
   - a. If word gets out that
   - b. Your secret's safe with me
   - c. I won't mention any names
   - d. I'll let you in on a little secret

5. This is serious. _____ we were responsible, we'll be in trouble.
   - a. If word gets out that
   - b. I don't want the whole world to know
   - c. Just between you and me
   - d. Your secret's safe with me

6. Don't worry – _____ .
   - a. you didn't hear this from me
   - b. off the record
   - c. your secret's safe with me
   - d. I don't want the whole world to know

7. OK, I'll tell you – but _____ .
   - a. if word gets out that
   - b. I'll let you in on a little secret
   - c. your secret's safe with me
   - d. I don't want the whole world to know

8. _____ , but I've decided to become a priest.
   - a. You didn't hear this from me
   - b. Off the record
   - c. Your secret's safe with me
   - d. I don't want this to get around

9. _____ , but John's decided to become a priest.
   - a. You didn't hear this from me
   - b. Off the record
   - c. Your secret's safe with me
   - d. I'll let you in on a little secret

10. I'll tell you what I think but this is strictly _____ .
    - a. I won't mention any names
    - b. you didn't hear this from me
    - c. off the record
    - d. I don't want this to get around

4 Dialogue Practice

1. Practice the dialogue in pairs.
2. Take turns being Margarita and Elias.
3. Practice until you can do the dialogue without reading it.
4. Do it for the class.

5 Role Play – 'The Daily Dirt'

'*The Daily Dirt*', a major tabloid newspaper, has discovered that you work as a house-keeper for Johnny Angelino, a famous actor. *The Daily Dirt* has come to your house asking for some personal information about your boss. The newspaper offered you a lot of money, so you gave them some information – but you were still afraid you would lose your job if Johnny found out who told them. Below is the article that appeared in *The Daily Dirt* the following day.

Using the article, and phrases from the dialogue, re-create the interview between you and the Daily Dirt reporter. Your partner will play the tabloid reporter and you will play the housekeeper. Make sure you take a few minutes to prepare and use all the phrases from the unit. Take turns playing each.

> ## Angelino – no angel!
>
> According to a reliable source, there are many aspects of Johnny Angelino's personal life the public does not know about. Mr. Angelino apparently has been having a secret ten-year relationship with a beautiful young woman – no names were mentioned. Also of interest is that Mr. Angelino snores at night and likes to read comic books. Surprisingly, says our inside informant, Mr. Angelino has never actually been to acting school, and only gets big roles in the films he stars in because he is a close friend of many major film producers and directors. On a funny note, it would appear that Johnny would also like to start a singing career, but our source says that his singing should be limited to the bathroom shower.

6 Discussion

Discuss in groups or with the class.

1. What do the following mean and how do they differ? Think of an example of each.

   to spread a rumor
   to overhear a conversation
   to talk behind someone's back
   to tell a secret
   to gossip
   to eavesdrop
   to be nosy

2. Can spreading a rumor be dangerous? Can it be hurtful?
3. At school / work: Do people talk behind other people's backs?
4. Is it always OK to tell a secret? When is it not OK? What is your experience?
5. Who gossips more – men or women? The same? Is the gossip of the same kind or different?

ANGRY WITH YOURSELF

Eddie's Disastrous Date

Nobody's perfect. We all make mistakes. And while it's not so common to show our anger towards others, it is very common to show anger with ourselves. It is a form of apology, a way of showing others that you recognize your own mistakes, and a good method of inserting humor into an uncomfortable situation. Eddie is having problems. Do you know anyone like him?

Eddie:	So, ... what do you think of my choice for a restaurant?
Daniela:	It's fine. Except. . . .
Eddie:	Except what?
Daniela:	It's just that I'm a vegetarian.
Eddie:	Oh no. I can't believe what an idiot I am! I should've known better than to take someone to Fred's Steak & Ribs on a first date. Me and my bright ideas.
Daniela:	That's OK.
	Daniela is staring at Eddie's ear.
Eddie:	What's the matter, Donna? Is something wrong?
Daniela:	(A *little upset*) It's Daniela. Anyway, you've got something white inside your ear.
	Eddie touches his left ear.
Daniela:	No – the other one.
	Eddie checks and then looks at his finger.
Eddie:	(*Blushing*) Oh great. Good one, Eddie.
Daniela:	(*Holding back her laughter*) What is it?
Eddie:	Shaving cream. I guess that's what I get for rushing, eh?
Daniela:	It's no big deal. I shouldn't have said anything. Me and my big mouth. Oh look . . . . here comes our order.

	A few minutes later.
Eddie:	How's your salad?
Daniela:	Fine. And your lobster? Eddie? Hello?
	Eddie is desperately trying to open something.

Eddie: What possessed me to order the lobster I'll never know. I'm sorry, Lynne. You were saying . . . .

Daniela: My name's D a n i e l a.

Eddie: Oops. What is it with me and names today? It's not like me to forget a person's name – especially one as pretty as yours.

Staring romantically into her eyes, Eddie reaches for Daniela's hand, but accidentally spills her glass of wine.

Daniela: Oh! You idiot! I can't believe I missed my niece's birthday party for *this*! What was I thinking? I'm going home. Thanks for . . . whatever this was.

Eddie: Would you like to join me for dessert at least?

Daniela: I think I'd rather be cut into little pieces and fed slowly to an alligator.

Eddie: Then I guess a goodnight kiss would be out of the question.

1 Phrase Jumble

Put the words in the correct order. All these expressions are used when you want to express anger or irritation with yourself.

1. Good Eddie one

   _____

2. Me big and mouth my

   _____

3. What thinking I was

   _____

4. I should've better known

   _____

5. What me with today it is and names

   _____

6. I believe I idiot what can't am an

   _____

7. It's like me forget not my to keys

   _____

8. Serves right the for lobster me ordering

   _____

9. I that's get for I what nice guess being

   _____

10. What me I'll possessed him never to marry know

    _____

Can you think of any more similar expressions which you would be happy using?

2 Situation-Phrase Match

Below are eleven things that happened to Mei-Ling on her day off, and the phrases that she used to react to these events. Two phrases are listed for each – only one is possible. Circle the one that is correct. Compare with a partner.

1. Mei-Ling dropped her pizza on the kitchen floor.
    a. I can't believe what a clumsy I am!
    b. I can't believe how clumsy I am!

2. Mei-Ling went to the bank, but it was closed.
    a. Today is Sunday! What was I thinking?
    b. Today is Sunday! What did I think?

3. Mei-Ling took a three-hour nap.
    a. It's not like me to sleep so much.
    b. It's not like me to sleeping so much.

4. Mei-Ling's friend told her that she had bad breath.
    a. I should know better than to eat garlic with my sardines.
    b. I should've known better than to eating garlic with my sardines.

5. Mei-Ling locked her keys inside her car.
    a. Very good one, Mei-Ling.
    b. Good one, Mei-Ling.

6. Mei-Ling got a stomach ache.
    a. Serves me right for to eat six bars of chocolate for lunch.
    b. Serves me right for eating six bars of chocolate for lunch.

7. Mei-Ling started a fire in her bedroom.
    a. I guess that's what I get for smoking in bed.
    b. I guess that's what I get for to smoke in bed.

8. Mei-Ling burned the chicken she had in the oven.
    a. What happens with me and food today?
    b. What is it with me and food today?

9. Mei-Ling's car broke down in the middle of the road.
    a. What possessed me to trust my brother-in-law to fix this, I'll never know.
    b. What possessed me to trust my brother-in-law to fix this, I never know.

10. Mei-Ling thought it would be fun to go to the park. It rained.
    a. Me and my big ideas.
    b. Me and my bright ideas.

11. Mei-Ling wanted to go for a walk, then remembered she promised her sister she would help her paint the house.
    a. My big mouth and me.
    b. Me and my big mouth.

3 Dialogue Practice

In pairs, one person play Daniela and the other, Eddie.

1. Read the dialogue sitting down.
2. Read it while physically acting out the scene. (You will need to do this a lot.)
3. Do it without the script as much as possible, until you feel comfortable.
4. Do it for the class. Whose is the most realistic?

4 Discussion

1. Have you or someone you know ever found yourself in an uncomfortable situation because you did something wrong? What happened?

2. Have you or someone you know ever put your foot in your mouth – said something you wish you hadn't? What was it? What did you do / say?

5 The Surprise Sentence Game

1. Your teacher will write the sentences and categories below on small bits of paper.

2. The class will be divided into two teams. A representative from each team will each pick up one bit of paper with one of the phrases written on it. The paper should be face-down. The teacher will pick up a different piece of paper – one with a category on it.

3. When the teacher says – Begin – you must try to make a conversation around the category, *and* include your sentence.

4. The one to use the sentence first *in a way that makes sense* is the winner.

Phrases

"I can't believe how stupid I've been."

"What was I thinking?"

"It's not like me to say such a stupid thing."

"I should know better."

"Good one, [your name]."

"Serves me right for believing what I see on T.V."

"I guess that's what I get for trying to do too much at the same time."

"What is it with me and grammar mistakes today?"

"What possessed me to buy a dog, I'll never know."

"Me and my big mouth."

"Me and my bright ideas."

Categories

What I did last summer	Food
Why I don't exercise	Cars
Something I've always wanted to do	Music
My best teacher	The first time I went swimming
Children	My biggest mistake

CONVERSATION TABOOS 3

Discuss

In English – perhaps more than in other languages – it is important to be able to avoid being too direct – particularly when speaking to a stranger. In your culture is it acceptable to speak to strangers? When? What topics could you talk about? Your family? Politics?

The Stranger

Something is not right with this conversation. With a partner, decide what should be changed.

Victim 1:	So then I told him, I said, "You have no business . . . ."
Stranger:	Hey, you! I heard you speaking English! Are you from England?
Victim 2:	No, we're not.
Stranger:	Well, then . . . where are you from?
Victim 1&2:	New Zealand.
Stranger:	Oh. I see you have cameras. You're on holiday.
Victim 1:	Yes, we are.
Stranger:	For how long?
Victim 2:	One week.
Stranger:	Only? Why so short?
Victim 1:	No time.
Stranger:	Oh, I see. Are you married?
Victim 1&2:	Yes, we are.
Stranger:	Do you have a big house in New Zealand?
Victim 2:	No, we don't.
Stranger:	Oh. Well, I won't be bringing my family to stay with you then, will I?

1 Re-write the Dialogue

With a partner, re-write the conversation. The phrases below will help you.

if you don't mind my asking　　　　　　*Not to interrupt, but . . .*
I couldn't help noticing . . .　　　　　　*It's really none of my business, but . . .*
I couldn't help overhearing　　　　　　*I hate to be nosy, but . . .*
I take it　　　　　　　　　　　　　　*I don't mean to be nosy, but . . .*
I was just wondering if . . .　　　　　　*Just out of curiosity, . . .*

Victim 1: _____

Stranger: _____

Victim 2: _____

Stranger: _____

Victim 1&2: _____

Stranger: _____

Victim 1: _____

Stranger: _____

Victim 2: _____

Stranger: _____

Victim 1: _____

Stranger: _____

Victim 1&2: _____

Stranger: _____

Victim 2: _____

Stranger: _____

When you finish:

1. ask the teacher for more suggestions
2. practice the new conversation with script
3. practice the new conversation without script
4. act out the new conversation
5. show the class

2 Role Play

A: Hey, it's you! Remember me?
B: No, I'm afraid I don't.

In pairs, decide:

1. Who is A?
2. Who is B?
3. Where are they?
4. Make a complete conversation until you reach a solution.
5. Your teacher will ask you to show the class.

3 Too Direct

Below are some ways of telling someone that you can't give them any of your time at the moment. Which would you interpret as rude?

1. Go away.
2. Can't you see I'm busy?
3. I'm afraid I can't right now.
4. Now isn't a good time.
5. You've picked a bad time.
6. Maybe now isn't a good time.
7. You couldn't have picked a worse time.
8. As if I didn't have enough things to do.
9. I'm busy.
10. Leave me alone.
11. Can I call you later?
12. Not now.
13. Perhaps another time.
14. I'll get back to you on that.
15. When hell freezes over.

Can you think of a situation where number 15 would be a possible reaction?

4 Role Play

Using the phrases above, work out a scene with a partner.

A: You need to talk to B about a problem at work.
B: You are very, very busy.

5 Discussion

1. When would you be able to speak to a total stranger?

2. What are some possible topics of conversation in the following situations:

    a. You are sitting beside someone on a ten-hour flight.

    b. You are sitting beside someone on a half-hour train ride.

    c. You are sharing a table with a stranger in a busy restaurant.

    d. You are waiting in line to see a film.

    e. You are in a hospital waiting room.

3. Can you improve the following opening sentences which a stranger might say to you:

    a. Are you going to tell me the time?

    b. So, where are you from then?

    c. Hey you, where's the train station?

    d. Help me with this suitcase.

    e. Why are you looking at me like that?

4. Have you ever had any weird conversations with a total stranger?

6 Openers

Here are some situations where it would be natural to speak to a stranger. How would you start the conversation? Try to write down the actual words you would use as an opening gambit. The first one is done for you as an example.

1. You are in the small waiting room of your dentist. A stranger is sitting opposite you. You have been waiting 20 minutes. The stranger is starting to look very white.

   Excuse me, are you feeling alright?

2. You are on vacation in Cairo, Egypt. You are in an elevator with two strangers – they are obviously Americans on vacation.

3. You are on vacation in Rome. You are in a line in a drugstore standing behind an elderly American trying to buy some painkillers. She cannot make herself understood. You speak fluent Italian.

4. You are alone on business in a different state. You go into a restaurant, but the only seat free is at a table with a stranger.

5. You are in a strange city on vacation. You need to go to the bathroom. You stop and ask a person in the street where the nearest one is.

6. You are two hours into a transatlantic flight. The person sitting next to you is of the opposite sex and looks really interesting. You are desperate to start a conversation.

7. Suddenly an elderly man slips and falls on the sidewalk in front of you. He is with a woman of roughly the same age. You offer to help.

8. You are returning to your parked car after doing some shopping. You see a couple of young hoodlums breaking into it. They have broken a side window and are trying to remove your car radio.

7 More Openers

Here are eight ways of starting a conversation with a person at a party. Which would you be prepared to use? Can you imagine what the replies might be?

1. Haven't we met before?
2. That's a lovely dress / color you're wearing.
3. I haven't talked to anyone for an hour. Please speak to me.
4. You look like the most interesting person here. What's your name?
5. I just love people with red hair. Are you Irish?
6. You look like you could do with another drink. Can I get you one?
7. I've been terrified to speak to you all evening. I'm Ron.
8. So . . . what brings you here?

SHARING PROBLEMS

English Troubles

One good way of letting a person know that you are listening is to use phrases to identify with the speaker – not necessarily to agree with the speaker, but to try to show that you are interested in what he or she is saying by responding. Tibor and Roberta are sharing a house in Sydney, Australia, where they are doing an English course. Can you relate to their complaints?

	Roberta walks in, throws her bag down, and slams the door behind her.
Tibor:	One of those days, huh?
Roberta:	Yeah. I'm just a little angry because no one seems to understand my English.
Tibor:	Oh, don't you hate that? Every time I go out people ask me, 'Where are you from?'
Roberta:	I hate when that happens. The other day I said 'Good morning' to the doorman and he said 'Buon giorno.' That really made me angry.
Tibor:	I can imagine. But if it makes you feel any better, this morning I had to ask the woman at the post office to write down the price for the stamps because I couldn't understand her accent.
Roberta:	Ouch. That must've been really embarrassing.
Tibor:	Very. I'm going to go to a different post office next time.
Roberta:	I don't blame you. Sometimes I wonder if my English will ever sound perfect.
Tibor:	Tell me about it.
Roberta:	Sometimes I feel like giving up.
Tibor:	I know the feeling. At first I felt like I was learning a lot, and now . . . . *(Tibor shakes his head)*
Roberta:	I know what you mean. I want to be treated as a native speaker of English – not as a woman from Italy.
Tibor:	Yeah, I can relate.
Roberta:	What?

1 Matching

In pairs, make a phrase by matching the correct word(s). Try to do it without the dialogue.

A

1. I hate when that	a. blame you.
2. One of those	b. relate.
3. I can	c. happens.
4. I don't	d. days, huh?
5. I can	e. imagine.

B

1. I know	f. about it.
2. That must've	g. the feeling.
3. Tell me	h. you mean.
4. Don't you	i. been terrible.
5. I know what	j. hate that?

All the above expressions are used when we want to identify with the speaker. Write them out now as complete expressions:

1. _____
2. _____
3. _____
4. _____
5. _____
6. _____
7. _____
8. _____
9. _____
10. _____

Now go back. Working in pairs, one person read the beginning of a phrase in the first column, and a partner completes it without looking.

2 Discussion

1. What things frustrate you about your English?

2. What do you find the most difficult to do in English?

3. What things do you like in your English classes? What things don't you like?

4. What kinds of teachers do you not like?

5. What do you like about the room you are in right now and what don't you like about it?

3 Pair Work

Which phrases from the dialogue can be used to respond to the following questions?

1. I locked the keys in my car.
    - a. I know what you mean.
    - b. I can imagine.
    - c. I hate when that happens.

2. That's the second time I've tripped and fallen today!
    - a. I can imagine.
    - b. One of those days, huh?
    - c. I don't blame you.

3. I miss home a lot.
    - a. I know what you mean.
    - b. That must've been horrible!
    - c. One of those days, huh?

4. I don't feel so well. I'm going to leave work early today.
    - a. I know what you mean.
    - b. I don't blame you.
    - c. That must've been awful!

5. I worked until three in the morning! I'm so tired.
    - a. I can imagine.
    - b. That must've been embarassing!
    - c. Don't you hate that?

6. Every time I eat popcorn I get thirsty.
    - a. Don't you hate that?
    - b. One of those days, huh?
    - c. That must've been embarassing!

7. He told me he had fallen in love with someone else.
    - a. I don't blame you.
    - b. Tell me about it.
    - c. That must've been awful!

8. I think I'm ugly and stupid.
    - a. I know the feeling.
    - b. I hate when that happens.
    - c. That must've been embarassing!

9. I'm tired of learning English.
    - a. Tell me about it.
    - b. One of those days, huh?
    - c. That must've been awful!

10. I understand most phrasal verbs but I'm too dumb to know how to use them.
    - a. I can relate.
    - b. I don't blame you.
    - c. I can imagine.

4 Dialogue Practice

1. Practice the dialogue in pairs.
2. Take turns being Roberta and Tibor.
3. Practice until you can do the dialogue without reading it.
4. Do it for the class.

5 Complaints

What would the following people complain about? In pairs, discuss and make notes. Choose _one_ only.

1. two beggars
2. the Queen of Britain and the President of the United States
3. two priests
4. a doctor and a dentist
5. two shoes salespeople
6. a waiter and a bartender
7. a famous TV actor and a film star
8. a couple of millionaires

6 Dialogue Building

Now, using what you thought of in exercise 5, create a dialogue between the two people you chose. Use as many of the phrases from this unit as you can. Do it in the following way: Write the dialogue on a piece of paper, passing the paper back and forth – each one writing a new line. Then practice what you have written. Finally, show the class.

7 Frustration

In a recent survey, people were asked what frustrates them most when going out to eat at a restaurant. Below are some things that were mentioned. In groups, put them in priority of most frustrating.

When the server brings the bill without you having asked for it first.

When a server takes a plate away when you still were not finished with it.

When the portions are too big.

When an item that appears on the menu is not available.

When a server spends five minutes of your time talking about the "Specials of the Day".

When you have to wait a long time to be waited on.

When they bring you the wrong order.

When orders are not served at the same time.

When food that is supposed to be served hot isn't.

When a server immediately asks the man of the table to try the wine first.

When you need to leave and you can't find the server to ask for the bill.

When a server ignores you during your meal.

When a server asks "How's everything?" with a ridiculous smile every three minutes.

When there's an insect in your salad.

When you have to ask for tableware (forks, knives, etc.)

Can you think of any others you could add? If you wanted to complain about some of these, what exact words would you use?

THE STATE OF THINGS

A Good Opportunity

To be able to talk about the state of things – if they are getting better or getting worse – is important. People often not only want to know how things are, but where they're going. Karen and Joseph are old friends. What is Karen worried about, and what solution does Joseph offer her?

Karen:	I'm not optimistic about finding a job after I finish college.
Joseph:	Oh? Why not?
Karen:	The economy is going downhill – fast.
Joseph:	I know. What is this world coming to? It's getting to the point where even a degree won't help you anymore.
Karen:	That's right. And the way things are going, I'll be lucky to even move out of my parents' house.
Joseph:	I know what you mean. First they raised taxes, then they cut education, and the salaries haven't gone up in years – it's just one thing after another.
Karen:	By the way, how's your business coming along?
Joseph:	Oh, it's getting there. Our sales are up only 2 percent, but it's a step in the right direction.
Karen:	I remember when you opened ten years ago and you almost went bankrupt. The company certainly has come a long way.
Joseph:	Yeah, but it's got a long way to go. Say, maybe you'd like to come work for me!
Karen:	Well, I'm not sure I want to work as a clothes-hanger inspector.
Joseph:	No . . . I mean as a manager.
Karen:	That's more like it.

1 Phrase Jumble

Put the words in the correct order. Re-write them.

1. It's there getting

   _____

2. That's it like more

   _____

3. It's downhill going

   _____

4. It's a long way come

   _____

5. It's got go to long way a

   _____

6. What's coming world to this?

   _____

7. It's the direction step a right in

   _____

8. It's thing another after one just

   _____

9. It's getting point the to where even a help won't degree

   _____

10. The way going are things college our won't to able be go to children

    _____

2 Discuss

1. Work with a partner. Sort the expressions in exercise 1 into two groups:
     those which mean *getting better*
     those which mean *getting worse*
2. Which phrases does your teacher use?
3. Have you heard any of them before?

3 Cloze 1

Below is part of a newspaper column. Fill in the missing parts with the phrases given. Use each phrase only once.

has come a long way   *it's getting to the point where*

What's this world coming to?   *the way things are going*

to be going downhill

Dear Ms. Etiquette

My husband and I are the proud parents of a 5 year-old boy and a newborn girl. I was brought up in a traditional family, so I know the importance of the presence and guidance of a parent. I have also noticed how the family in today's society seems 1._____ because parents are "unable" to stay home because of demanding careers. Keeping this in mind, my husband and I have decided that he will work and I will stay home to look after the children. I now wonder if what I am doing is the right thing because everyone is accusing me of being a "slave" to my husband! 2._____
I believe in women's rights but 3._____ we seem to have lost our sense of good judgement over those rights. I believe the woman in our modern world 4._____ and can now can be liberated *and* be a good mother. I also want to be a good mother, but 5._____
I might have to decide between sticking to my beliefs and the possibility of losing my friends.
What do you think?
The Good Mother

---

4 Cloze 2

Below is part of the reply to the letter in Cloze 1. Fill in the missing parts with the phrases given. Use each phrase only once.

we've got a long way to go	*it's getting there*
a step in the right direction	*that's more like it*
just one thing after another	

Dear Good Mother,

I understand what you are saying but I cannot agree with you. Yes, women have more rights now than they used to but 1. _____. I understand that you want to give your children the best home possible, but you should not do it if it means sacrificing a career. I did that once in my life and I will never do it again. The moment I let him tell me what to do with my professional life he started dictating when I could go out, and who I could talk to, and it was 2. _____ until finally we got a divorce a few years later. Perhaps being a working mother is not the solution to all of women's problems today, but it's certainly 3. _____. I am now re-married with a baby on the way. My husband respects my career and, while our marriage may not be perfect (yet), 4._____, and I will never again give anyone my freedom. A proud parent AND a proud professional. Now 5._____ .

By the way, which person do you agree with more and why?

5 Dialogue Practice

1. Practice the dialogue in pairs.
2. Take turns being Karen and Joseph.
3. Practice until you can do the dialogue without reading it.
4. Do it for the class.

6 Pair Work

One of the commonest topics of conversation is the past – our memories, and what things used to be like. Work in pairs and talk about some of your earliest memories. Here are some expressions to try to use:

I used to	In those days . . . .
Things aren't what they used to be.	Back then . . . .
Things used to be cheaper / better / safer etc	Back in the (60's) . . . .
I don't know what things are coming to.	I mean, whatever happened to . . . .
When I was a boy / girl	There was once a time when . . . .
People didn't used to	
People today just don't	

Now report back in the whole class some of the important points you discussed in pairs.

7 Discussion

Using phrases from this unit, discuss at least one of the following subjects in pairs. Use the following questions:

1. What is the situation like now in your country?
2. What was it like before?
3. What do you see in the future?

VIOLENT CRIME	DRUG ADDICTION	**EDUCATION**
WOMEN'S RIGHTS	**THE ENVIRONMENT**	HEALTH CARE
THE FAMILY	RACIAL TOLERANCE	**HOMELESSNESS**
	GOVERNMENT CORRUPTION	

After discussing in pairs, tell the rest or your class what you talked about. Remember to use the phrases you have practiced.

8 Headlines

Here are some headlines taken from newspapers. Work first in pairs and try to decide what the stories were about. Then come together as the whole class and compare your stories:

1. Let public get the facts
2. Missing child is found dead
3. Victim of fatal shark attack survives fire
4. Fire guts home in City Heights
5. Democrat faces fraud charges
6. Jailed killer still preying on people
7. Missing-child group to fold
8. Battling Nightmare Neighbors
9. Trial's New Phase
10. 19 injured in solvent explosion
11. Fall hospitalizes Disneyland visitor
12. Wilson urges life term for first offense
13. Gang unit probes wounding of teen
14. Gun control measures to go forward
15. Tobacco firms face showdown
16. Shuttle back safely
17. Priest may have been bomb target
18. Russia won't budge
19. Brothers found not guilty in Fire Deaths of 4
20. Innocent bystanders killed

Here are some more headlines taken from newspapers. They all contain something amusing. What is funny about each one?

21. FLAMING TOILET SEAT CAUSES EVACUATION AT HIGH SCHOOL
22. TRAFFIC DEAD RISE SLOWLY
23. IRAQI HEAD SEEKS ARMS
24. ROBBER HOLDS UP ALBERT'S HOSIERY
25. DRUNK GETS NINE MONTHS IN VIOLIN CASE
26. QUEEN MARY HAVING BOTTOM SCRAPED
27. JUDGE TO RULE ON NUDE BEACH
28. LAWYERS GIVE POOR FREE LEGAL ADVICE

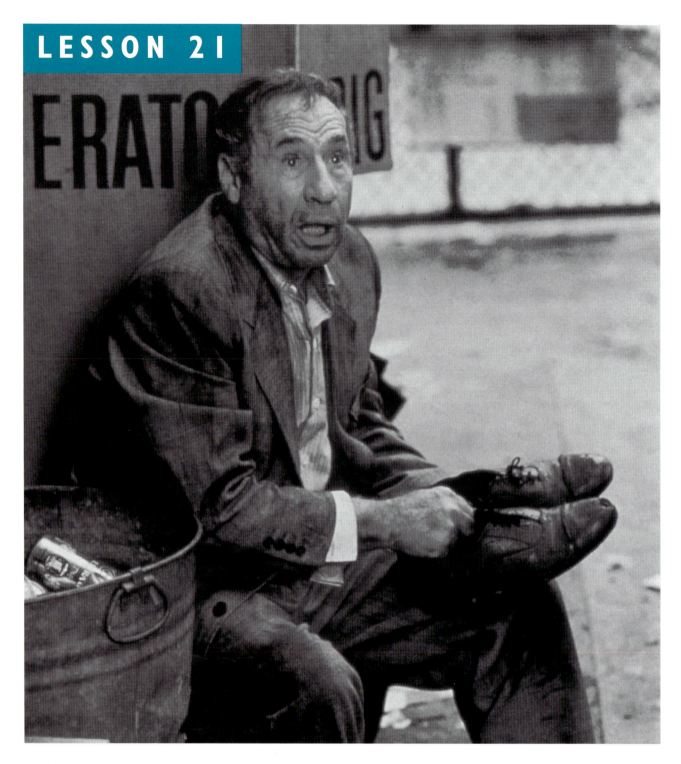

CONVERSATION FRAME 4

Dale is not impressed.

Dale has some serious problems. What are they?

Josephine:	I brought you the new Groove People CD.
Dale:	What good is a CD if I haven't got a CD player?
Josephine:	I can bring you a CD player.
Dale:	What good is a CD player if I don't even have electricity?
Josephine:	Why don't you call the Electric Company?
Dale:	What good is calling the Electric Company if I haven't got a house?

1 Mary who has everything

Mary has everything she could ever want in her big house in Toronto. But Mary lives in Vancouver. Below is a list of things Mary has in her house in Toronto.

a guitar	three nephews	an enormous bed
a swimming pool	a video collection	a loving husband
a leather sofa	lots of expensive wine	closets full of designer clothes
a huge collection of CD's	piles of fantastic books	a beautiful garden

Mary's friends ask her:

What good is having a big house in Toronto if you don't live in it?

Can you make 12 more sentences like this one using the other things Mary has in her house? Work with a partner.

What good is having _____ in Toronto if you _____ .

2 Problem Gifts

A CD was the wrong gift for Dale. Work in pairs. You are two friends looking for a wedding gift. Take turns being B.

A: You propose some gift ideas.
B: You know the couple, and will find something wrong with every idea A proposes.
For example:
    A: *Oh! I know! We can get them an ice cream maker.*
    B: *What good is an ice cream maker when we know that Bill is on a fat free diet!*

> **Some useful expressions for A:**
>
> What do you think about . . .
> I think they would like . . .
> Oh! I know! We can get them . . .
> What about a . . .

Some gift ideas:

a computer	a cassette player	a dog
a baby buggy	a television	a vacuum cleaner
a piano	a set of bed sheets	a coffee maker
a bookcase	camping gear	a set of skis

Now think of some more amusing gift ideas and try to make the rest of your class laugh. Vote on which conversation is best.

3 Discussion

1. Have you ever been to a wedding? Did you have to bring a gift?
2. In your country, what are some good (or typical) wedding gifts?
3. What if you've been invited to a party – should you bring a gift? If so, what kind?

4 Game – Dale's Problem

Dale could not listen to the CD because he did not have a CD player, and he did not have a CD player because he had no electricity, and he had no electricity because he did not even have a house. Here is a game to play round the class.

Teacher or student say:	*You should learn to drive.*
Next student begins:	*What good is learning to drive if I don't have a car.*
Then the next says:	*And what good is having a car if I don't even have a place to go.*
And the same student then starts a new one.	
	Did you brush your teeth?
Then the next says:	*What good is brushing my teeth if I don't have any?*
. . . and so on.	

The person who can't think of something to add is out. Here are some conversation openers to help you:

You should learn to drive	Do you have a credit card?
Did you go to college?	Do you know the time?
Are you married?	Want to go to a disco?
You ought to see a doctor	You need a vacation
You ought to have your hair done	Maybe you should sleep

5 Your Problems

Use this frame to fill in some things that are true about yourself:

What good is   **if I**

6 Discussion

Look back at the picture on page 86. What is the situation? Are there any people like that where you live? What should we do about them? Here are two very different points of view. Which is closest to your own opinion?

A

In our town there are a number of down and outs who hang around the train station. It gives a very bad impression of our town when visitors arrive and what do they see but winos and good-for-nothings. Now I know that some of these guys can't help themselves. Some are veterans, and some should be in institutions if there was an institution that would have them, but some of them are able-bodied men who could work if they had a mind to do it. I think we have to start a national program to get them back to work. It doesn't matter what work. They could work in trash collection, for instance. We should round them all up and take them away to a center where they can be cleaned up, see a doctor and a dentist and be given clean clothes and somewhere decent to live for a while so that they can learn again how to live with other people. We should put them back in contact with their families and make their families take some of the responsibility for them. God, I don't know what I'd do if I was in their position, but if someone handed me the chance to start again, I'd jump at it.

B

Every man you pass lying on the sidewalk is a live human being with all the hopes and desires for life that we have. They deserve better from the rest of us. Most of us just don't want to know – and we pass by on the other side – we even look down on people who give them money. But these men were once loved and valued. Someone you once knew might be there – a relative or an old classmate. Just to let them lie there is one of our society's worst crimes. We are sick when we hear what Hitler did. We give money to help badly treated animals, but what do we do for these poor people? Nothing. It is a scandal and we cannot escape from it. We are responsible for them. We should be taking them into our church halls and feeding them; we should be taking them into our homes and clothing them. Above all, we should be getting to know them. Let's all start today. Stop and talk to them. Ask them how you can help them. If they want money, give it to them. Lobby your Town Hall. Write to Congress. Start a campaign today.

BEING NEGATIVE
The Information Booth

Mark, Marcia, and Henry work at the Information Desk of a train station. Should they consider a career change?

Traveler:	Excuse me – do you know when the next train arrives?
Mark:	Good question. Marcia, Do you know when the next train arrives?
Marcia:	You got me. How about you, Henry?
Henry:	How should I know?
Mark:	(*to Traveler*) Sorry – we have no idea.
Traveler:	Well, then maybe you could tell me when the last one leaves.
Mark:	Well, it's anyone's guess, really.
Marcia:	Yeah. Who's to say?
Henry:	That's right. There's no telling.
Mark:	(*to Traveler*) You see.
Traveler:	How did you people get a job working at the Information Booth of a train station?
Mark:	Don't ask me.
Marcia:	Who knows?
Henry:	Your guess is as good as mine.

1 Phrase Correction

Each phrase below has a small error. Circle the mistakes, check with a partner, then re-write the correct phrases below.

1. I haven't an idea.
_____

2. Your guess is so good as mine.
_____

3. It's everyone's guess.
_____

4. Who know?
_____

5. There's no saying.
_____

6. Who's to tell?
_____

7. You get me.
_____

8. A good question.
_____

9. Don't ask to me.
_____

10. How must I know?
_____

2 Pair Work

Ask your partner the following questions. S/he may answer with any phrase from this unit, but it must be a different phrase for each question. Try it without looking at the phrases!

1. Do you think there is life in outer space?

2. How come he didn't finish his education?

3. What's the capital of Cameroon?

4. Do you think we'll ever see an end to world hunger?

5. What's 3,425,799 divided by 81.52?

6. Mommy...Why did you marry Daddy?

7. I wonder why we exist?

8. What'll the weather be like tomorrow?

9. What's the time?

10. I wonder why he's late this time?

Can the meaning of a phrase change when you change the pronunciation? Can you give an example?

3 Trivia Game

How good are you at trivia? Try the following quiz in pairs, then compare your answers with the class.

1. What is the official language of the United States of America?
2. Name the four band members of The Beatles.
3. What sports use a bat?
4. What does UFO stand for?
5. Can you name eight countries where English is spoken as a first language?
6. In America, he is called "Santa Claus". What is he called in the U.K.?
7. How many states are there in the U.S.A.?
8. What is the only man-made structure visible from space?
9. Name five works written by William Shakespeare.
10. What can contain more liquid: A one-gallon jug or a one-gallon pitcher?
11. How many continents are there in the world?
12. Where can you find the Golden Gate Bridge?
13. What is the former capital of Japan?
14. The White House is in Washington D.C. Where is "The Pink House"?
15. What is the opposite of a smile?

4 Dialogue Practice

1. Practice the dialogue in groups of four.
2. Choose parts, then read the scene.
3. Act out the scene while reading the script.
4. Memorize the dialogue and perform it.

5 Role Play

Form groups of five to ten people. One person in each group is a football coach who has to substitute for a teacher. The rest of the group is the class who have to ask him / her questions about the subject of the class! Act out the question session. Take turns being the substitute teacher.

The Football Coach
Choose which teacher you are going to substitute for from the list below. If you cannot answer the students' questions, show your ignorance by using the expressions from the dialogue.

Mathematics	Science
History	Human Biology
English	Economics
Religion	Geography

The Students
Your teacher is off sick. The football coach is the substitute teacher. Ask him / her questions about the subject of the lesson. Each student should prepare at least two questions in advance.

6 Discussion

You have a five-year-old daughter who is very curious. Which of the following questions would you answer honestly? Show your answers to a partner, then to the class.

1. Is there really a Santa Claus?
2. How was I born?
3. Are you the smartest mommy / daddy in the whole world?
4. Do you always tell me the truth?
5. Who do you love more – me or mommy / daddy?
6. Were you always a good student in school?
7. Can I be whoever I want to be when I grow up?
8. Why do people die?
9. Are you the best mommy / daddy in the world?
10. Did you ever like someone else besides mommy / daddy?

7 What do you say?

The man in the train station got very bad service from the staff in the information booth. What do you do when you experience bad service? Do you complain or just shrug it off because you don't like making a fuss? Here are some very different situations. What would you say in each?

1. You have been waiting to check in at the hotel reception desk for ten minutes. During all of that time the reception staff have been chatting in the room behind the reception area. The door has been slightly open, so you know they have been gossiping about the hotel manager. At last one of the staff comes out and says *Can I help you, sir*?

2. You and your spouse are staying in a very expensive hotel with your 25 year old son. Your son is very young-looking for his age. Most people think he is 18 years old. Yesterday in the bar he ordered a drink and was asked to prove his age. You are in the bar with him today and a different barman has just asked him to prove his age again. He has left his identity card in his room.

3. You have just been shopping and have bought a new and very expensive sweater. You got home, opened the parcel, and you are sure that the sweater has been worn by someone – there is a strong smell of sweat on it. You take it back for a refund.

4. You and your elderly mother are having a meal. The food has just arrived. There is a very long hair in her pasta dish. She doesn't want to make a fuss, but you know she is upset about it. You decide to get her a new dish.

5. You have just got on the plane for a 12 hour flight to Tokyo. An extremely overweight person comes and sits down in the seat next to you. You are extremely uncomfortable, and the plane hasn't taken off yet. What do you say to the attendant whom you have just summoned.

LESSON 23

GUESSING

Car Problems

Rosie has brought her car to Paul, her mechanic. Would you trust Paul with your car?

Rosie:	OK, Paul . . . What do you think it is?
Paul:	Well, knowing these German imports, my guess is it's the engine.
Rosie:	Could you be more specific?
Paul:	Well, if I had to take a guess, I'd say it's the fuel system.
Rosie:	How much is that going to be?
Paul:	Well, chances are it's going to be pretty expensive.
Rosie:	How much is expensive?
Paul:	Just off the top of my head, I'd say around a thousand – but it's hard to say.
Rosie:	You're kidding. And how long is this going to take?
Paul:	Oh, we're talking maybe a month. I would even go as far as to say two months.
Rosie:	Why does it seem there's always something wrong with this car?
Paul:	Well, it could be that it's time for you to get a new car.
Rosie:	I would say that it has more to do with that new car you just bought.
Paul:	Maybe.

1 What's the Phrase?

Using the cues, complete the phrase.

1. _____ talking maybe a month.

2. _____ say he's about forty or so.

3. Chances _____ she'll never come back.

4. My _____ _____ she's not happy at her job.

5. _____ could be _____ it's time to get a new car.

6. He may be out sick today, but _____ _____ _____ say.

7. _____ these German imports, it's probably a problem with the brakes.

8. I would even _____ _____ _____ _____ _____ _____ two months.

9. _____ _____ _____ _____ _____ _____ guess, I'd say he's married.

10. _____ _____ _____ _____ _____ _____ head, I don't how much it'll be.

Now go back and underline the phrases used for guessing.

2 Pair Work

1. True or false: *we're talking maybe* is used when guessing quantity.

2. Which phrase is used when taking a guess that may seem extreme?
   - a. If I had to guess, I would say that they're from Scotland.
   - b. Chances are they're from Scotland.
   - c. I would even go as far as to say they're from Scotland.

3. Which phrase is not a guess: *Just off the top of my head,*
   - a. I saw Christy do it.
   - b. I'd say Christy did it.
   - c. I think Christy did it.

4. Which expression is a guess based on a generalization?

5. In the box below, circle the combinations that are **not** possible.

> a. **If I had to take a guess,**
> b. **My guess is,**
> c. **Chances are,**   **I'd say she caught the last train.**
> d. **Knowing my mother,**
> e. **Just off the top of my head,**

6. Which is the best answer to the question?
   - A: How old do you think I am?

     B: I would say you're about thirty-six.
   - *or...*   B: It could be that you're about thirty-six.

3 Dialogue Practice

1. Practice the dialogue in pairs.
2. Take turns being each character.
3. Practice until you can do the dialogue without reading it.
4. Do it for the class.

4 Trivia – What do you know about the USA?

This quiz is based on a United Air In-Flight Travel Magazine. Mark the following True or False.

1.	The capital of California is San Francisco.	T	F
2.	There are three official languages in the USA.	T	F
3.	A student finishes high school at 18.	T	F
4.	In the US, one must be 16 to drive.	T	F
5.	In the US, one must be 20 to drink alcohol.	T	F
6.	The first president was Abraham Lincoln.	T	F
7.	Puerto Rico was the last state admitted into the Union.	T	F
8.	The national hymn is "God Bless America."	T	F
9.	Guns are legal.	T	F
10.	The death penalty is legal in all states.	T	F
11.	McDonald's invented the hamburger.	T	F
12.	Albert Einstein was an American.	T	F

Check your answers with a partner and then with the class. Were you surprised at any of the answers?

5 Guessing Expressions

There are a number of expressions which we use especially when guessing. Fill in the following words to complete them:

hunch   *bones*   *sixth*   *intuition*   *feeling*

1. I have a _____ it's too late to do anything about it.
2. I feel it in my _____ .
3. Call it women's _____ if you like! It's what I think is going to happen!
4. My _____ sense tells me it's going to be a good year for trout.
5. I have a _____ they'll get in for another term.

What is the last sentence about?

6 Guessing Game – What do you know?

What do you know about your classmates? Working alone, write down the answers to these questions on a separate piece of paper.

1. What's your favorite color?
2. What's your favorite food?
3. How many countries have you visited?
4. Do you have any brothers or sisters?
5. Have you ever eaten at McDonald's?
6. Do you prefer the British or the American accent?
7. Do you have some computer skills?
8. Do you consider yourself intelligent? How would you rate yourself on a scale of 1 to 10?
9. How long have you been studying English?
10. What's your astrological sign?

When finished, give your paper to another student. Then, work in pairs (not with the same student whose answers you have) asking questions like this:

Chisato: *What do you think Yuji's favorite food is?*
Arlette: *Well, knowing Yuji, he probably only likes Japanese food.*
Chisato: *You're right.*
Arlette: *How many countries do you think Markus has visited?*

7 Discussion

The following letter appeared recently:

> Dear Editor
>
> I don't like my job anymore. I used to have friends here I could count on and I used to know the people around me. I don't like my neighborhood anymore, because I don't like my neighbors anymore. They're not like me. Everyone around me is different. Who let these people in here, anyway? This country is losing its identity, its traditions, its customs. These people don't belong here. Let them go back to where they came from. People these days say my ideas and view of the world are old-fashioned and out-of-date. But wanting to have a place to live where your friends and neighbors are like you – is that being old-fashioned? If so, then so be it. I'll live my life my way, let them live it theirs.
>
> J. Anderson

1. Would you say that the person who wrote this letter is a man or a woman?
2. How old would you say the person is?
3. What race would you say the person is?
4. What would you say the person is complaining about exactly?
5. Why do you think this person feels this way?

CONVERSATION TABOOS 4

The Deadline

There are those who are able to work very efficiently all the time and never waste a minute. And then there are those of us who are human and miss deadlines, work unsteadily and make mistakes. Something is not right with this conversation. With a partner, decide what should be changed.

Boss:	Clint! Have you finished that report?
Clint:	I've been too lazy to do it.
Boss:	When will it be done?
Clint:	No later than next year – if you're lucky.
Boss:	Why so long?
Clint:	I don't want to tell you.
Boss:	And the proposal?
Clint:	I haven't even thought about it.
Boss:	When can you have it finished?
Clint:	Probably never.
Boss:	Also, I want you to make plans for an entire new building by tomorrow morning.
Clint:	That's absolutely impossible. I'm sure I won't do it.
Boss:	How long will it take?
Clint:	Forever.

1 Re-write the Dialogue

With a partner, re-write the conversation. The phrases below will help you.

I'll see what I can do.   *It shouldn't be long.*   *I'll do the best I can.*   *It's a long story.*
Should be any day now.   *I'm working on it.*   *It may take a while.*   *I haven't got around to it yet.*

Boss: _____

Clint: _____

Boss: _____

Clint: _____

Boss: _____

Clint: _____

Boss: _____

Clint: _____

Boss: _____

Clint: _____

Boss: _____

Clint: _____

Boss: _____

Clint: _____

When you finish:

1. Ask the teacher for more suggestions.
2. Practice the new conversation with, then without script.
3. Act out the new conversation, then show the class.

2 Role Play

A: Mr/s Ward! Do you have your homework?   **B: Sorry . . . can I bring it tomorrow?**
In pairs, decide:

1. Who is A? Who is B?
2. Where are they?
3. Make a complete conversation until you reach a solution.
4. Your teacher will ask you to show the class.

3 Who said it?

Some of the things below were said by Ed, a super-worker, and others were said by Ken, who is lazy and procrastinates. In pairs, decide who said what.

1. I'll be there in a minute.
2. I'll get to it tomorrow.
3. It was about time.
4. It's long overdue.
5. I'll do it first thing in the morning.
6. There's no better time than the present.
7. I'll have it ready for you first thing in the morning.
8. Yeah, sooner or later.
9. We've got plenty of time.
10. It'll just take a second.
11. I can't work on an empty stomach.
12. That's pushing it, I think.
13. It should be no problem.
14. I'll make it up to you.

Now work out another scene like the first one between Clint and his boss. If you were a small business owner, what qualities would you look for in an employee?

AVOIDING COMMITMENT

The New Girl

Conrad and Ken are in the employee's lounge. What is their mistake and why do they make it?

Conrad:	Hey . . . . Who's the new girl?
Ken:	Well, from what I understand she's the new secretary. Cute, huh?
Conrad:	Very. But, my understanding was that they were hiring some guy from the other department.
Ken:	I'm just going by what they've told me.
Conrad:	Well, I'm no expert, but that outfit she's wearing doesn't look cheap.
Ken:	Well, from what I hear she has expensive tastes in both clothes and men.
Conrad:	So who's going to be the new supervisor?
Ken:	From what I gathered they've got somebody from the outside – but don't quote me on that.
Conrad:	Really? I wonder who.
Ken:	As far as I know he hasn't shown up yet – but I could be wrong. Hey, look! Here comes that cute new girl.
'Cute Girl':	Good morning, gentlemen. I don't believe we've met. My name's Therese.
Ken:	Hi, Therese. Are you the new secretary?
Therese:	[*visibly upset*] Actually, the way I understand it is that I'll be your new supervisor.
Ken &Conrad:	Oh.

1 Phrase Correction

Each phrase below has a small error. Re-write each phrase correctly, then check with a partner.

1. but don't quote me for that

   _____

2. I'm not expert, but

   _____

3. I'm just going to what they've told me.

   _____

4. from that I understand

   _____

5. from what I'll gather

   _____

6. but I can be wrong

   _____

7. as far from I know

   _____

8. from what I listen

   _____

9. my comprehension was

   _____

10. the way I understand

    _____

Now add the correct phrase to these sentences:

The way I quote me	I hear gather	As far expert	From what wrong	going by understanding

11. _____ understand it the wedding is to be held in June.

12. _____ as I know I'm next to be promoted to Vice President.

13. _____ I understand, he won't be returning until next week.

14. I don't know if it's true . . . . I'm just _____ what they told me

15. I'm no _____ but I think the Super Bowl is played in January.

16. São Paolo is the biggest, but I could be _____ .

17. The weather there is really nice, from what _____ .

18. My _____ was that you knew our system already.

19. From what I _____ they haven't seen each other in months.

20. I'm pretty sure it's $150, but don't _____ on that.

2 Pair Work

1. Which verbs can come after the phrase *'from what I...'*? Are the meanings different for each phrase? Are there other possible verbs you can think of?

2. What phrase in the dialogue is like *'...but I could be wrong'*?

3. What word usually comes after *'I'm no expert'*? Why is this word important to this phrase?

4. True or False: When someone says *'my understanding is/was'* or *'the way I understand it'*, that person is implying that they got that information from someone else.

5. How is *'as far as I know'* different from *'as long as I know'*?

6. Which one – a or b – is closest in meaning to *'I'm just going by what they've told me'* ?
   a. "Just in case the information I am giving is wrong, let me tell you that someone else told me."
   b. "I am repeating what someone else has told me, so what I am saying is really not new information."

3 Dialogue Practice

1. Practice the dialogue in groups of three.
2. Take turns being Ken, Conrad, and Therese.
3. Practice until you can do the dialogue without reading it.
4. Do it for the class.

4 Apparently

The word *apparently* is another very useful word used quite frequently to express being non-committal. Working with a partner, put an arrow (^) wherever you think *apparently* can go in the dialogues below.

1. A: I want to go skiing this weekend. There's been a lot of snow.
   B: Yeah, but it's not very good.
   A: They've put some artificial snow there now.
   B: Oh, I didn't know that

2. A: Have you seen Marcel around lately?
   B: He's been sick.
   A: Oh, really? There's something going around.
   B: Yeah, some kind of flu.

3. A: What do you know about the TOEFL exam?
   B: It's very difficult.
   A: You have to get a minimum score of 550.
   B: The listening part is the most difficult.

Compare your answers with others in the class. Practice the dialogues in pairs.

5 Role Play – Dirt Cheap Travel Agency

Working in pairs, take turns being a travel agent and a customer.

Travel agent

It's only your first week on the job. You have never really traveled anywhere – ever. Using expressions from the dialogue, try to sell some tours.

Customer

You are desperate to travel, and it doesn't matter where you go as long as it's far away. You have never really traveled before, but you have heard about a few places. Use expressions learned in this unit.

For example:

Travel agent: *So, do you know where you'd like to go?*

Customer: *Do you have any suggestions?*

Travel agent: *Well, from what I hear Vancouver's great.*

Customer: *Actually, my understanding was that it's too expensive and it's cold all the time.*

Travel agent: *Well, yes, but apparently . . .*

6 Discussion – Would you buy it?

College in a Book

Newhouse Press
$19.95 (Hardback)
Have you ever felt intimidated in a crowd of highly-educated individuals? Well, fear no more – **College in a Book** now brings you an education you can walk away from the bathroom with. For just $19.95, you'll be able to converse on subjects like: philosophy, world history, science, art, politics, literature, economy, finance, theology and much, much more! Never again feel afraid to talk with the academics at a conference or other social gathering. Impress your friends! Impress a mate! Act now before it's too late.

1. Would you buy this book? Why or why not?
2. Who are the advertisers trying to sell this book to?
3. What devices do the advertisers use to try to persuade the reader to buy the book?

TERMINATION

Helga the Health-Nut

Helga and Bruno are in the park. How long in total do they exercise?

Helga:	Let's get this over with.
Bruno:	Yeah. We'd better or we'll end up just going for coffee like the last time.
Helga:	One hour, right?
Bruno:	That's right.
	Ten minutes later...
Helga:	(*out of breath*) Well I'm ready to call it quits. How about you?
Bruno:	(*also out of breath*) So much for one hour.
Helga:	OK. Let's go ten more minutes and then we're through, OK?
	Five minutes later...
Bruno:	How many minutes have we been running?
Helga:	Five.
Bruno:	Five down and five to go.
	Two minutes later...
Helga:	Time's up! Well, that's it for me.
Bruno:	Yeah, that should just about do it.
Helga:	Next time we'll go for an hour and a half. I'm feeling healthier already!
Bruno:	On that note, let's go for a cheeseburger.
Helga:	Good idea.

1 Matching

In pairs, make a phrase by matching the correct word(s). Try to do it without the dialogue.

1. Let's get this	_____	a. up
2. As usual, we'll end	_____	b. to go
3. That should just about	_____	c. quits
4. I'm through	_____	d. over with
5. So much	_____	e. note, I'll say goodbye
6. Time's	_____	f. do it
7. Five down and two	_____	g. it for me
8. On that	_____	h. up going back to his place
9. Well, that's	_____	i. for the millionaire lifestyle!
10. Let's call it	_____	j. for the day.

Use five of these phrases to respond in these situations:

11. So, how long have you been at medical school?

_____

12. Come on! Give me another 30 seconds!

_____

13. Where will you go after the performance?

_____

14. I was going to marry her because I thought she was rich!

_____

15. Wait . . . I owe you another beer.

_____

2 Who said it?

With a partner, decide who could have said the following.

1. OK, let's get this over with . . . short on the sides but keep it long in the back.
2. If you don't stop eating you'll end up like your father.
3. No, that should just about do it for today. Actually, give me another baguette.
4. So much for the veggie burgers. Anyone have a fire extinguisher?
5. Time's up! Put your pencils down and pass your tests forward.
6. On that note, let's break for lunch.
7. Let's call it quits. We'll paint the doors and window-sills tomorrow.
8. Well, that's it for today. Please join us tomorrow for more "Inside Politics".
9. Only three months to go and we don't even know if it's a boy or a girl.
10. Are you through with your plate, sir?

3 Pair Work

Work in pairs. Discuss the following questions. Then see if the whole class can agree.

1. How is *Let's get this over with* different from *Let's call it quits*?

2. If someone says, looking out the window: "Well, so much for a picnic.", what is probably happening?

3. If you drink too much alcohol, how do you usually end up? And what do people usually end up doing with the left-over food in the refrigerator?

4. You are looking forward to finishing college (four years). You have just completed your third year. What phrase might be appropriate?

5. You have given your friend exactly one minute to solve a puzzle. You look at your watch and fifty-nine seconds have passed. In a second you are going to say: _____ .

6. A: "I don't think it's perfect, but I'll admit it has improved immensely."
   B: _____ .
   C: "Yes, good idea. We can resume discussion then, and we **are** all getting a bit hungry, I think."
   What did B probably say?

7. Which phrase means: "I think, more or less, that there is no more to do."

8. Fill in the blank: "and _____ boys' names. Now, do you have any suggestions if it's a girl?"

9. True or False: When someone says, 'I have to wrap up this report', it means they are almost finished.

4 Questionnaire

Are you a procrastinator? To find out, complete the questionnaire below and show it to a partner.

1. When I receive bills in the mail I:
   a. Open and pay them right away
   b. Wait until I get paid before I look at them
   c. Open them, but pay them when it is convenient

2. When I say, "Let's get together sometime.", I mean:
   a. I will definitely call to make arrangements for us to meet
   b. "Goodbye"
   c. There's a good chance I'll at least call you

3. I receive a letter from someone I met on a trip:
   a. I read the letter and send a reply the same day
   b. I open the letter and skim it, think about sending a reply but never do
   c. I read the letter and wait till I have something to say, then I write

4. I do most of my housework:
   a. Monday through Thursday
   b. On the weekends
   c. Whenever I get the chance

5. I hit the 'snooze' button on my alarm clock:
    a. Never
    b. Always
    c. Sometimes

6. I do my food shopping:
    a. On a regular basis
    b. If the refrigerator is empty
    c. When I start running out of things to eat

7. The last time I went to the dentist was (at the most):
    a. Six months ago
    b. Dentist?
    c. A year or so ago . . . I think

5 Dialogue Practice

1. Practice the dialogue in pairs.
2. Take turns being Helga and Bruno.
3. Practice until you can do the dialogue without reading it (at some point you will have to pretend you are running).
4. Do it for the class.

6 Expansion

Below are some fixed phrases that are also related to termination.

1. His hair is	_____	a. flat
2. My patience is wearing	_____	b. expired
3. The party is winding	_____	c. broke
4. The storm is beginning to	_____	d. end
5. The date has already	_____	e. thin
6. The light bulb burned	_____	f. deal
7. Drink the beer before it goes	_____	g. thinning
8. The street came to a dead	_____	h. subside
9. I'm afraid I'm flat	_____	i. down
10. They're ready to close the	_____	j. out

7 Last-line Dialogues

Working in groups of two or three, make a dialogue using one of the phrases from Exercise 6. The last line of the dialogue must be one of the following phrases:

1. "We ended up taking it off."
2. "Let's get this over with."
3. ". . . . so on that note, I'll leave you with the keys to my Ferrari."
4. "That's it for the little ones. Now, how about those big ones over there?"
5. "Time's up!"
6. "That's two down, and ninety-eight to go."
7. "So much for modern technology."
8. "Let's call it quits."
9. "Let's eat one more and then we'll wrap it up."
10. "Just put the nose on and that should just about do it."

CONVERSATION FRAME 5

Self Defense

For every negative thing John has to say, Doug can say something positive:

John:	Your car is ugly.
Doug:	It may be ugly, but at least it can go fast.
John:	Your house is small.
Doug:	It may be small, but at least it's warm.
John:	Your dog barks too much.
Doug:	My dog may bark too much, but at least makes a great security system.

Using the same pattern, continue with a partner.

John:	Your shoes are ugly.
Doug:	1. _____
John:	Your coat is not very nice.
Doug:	2. _____
John:	You're old.
Doug:	3. _____
John:	I think you're boring.
Doug:	4. _____
John:	The buses in this city are dirty.
Doug:	5. _____
John:	You spend too much time exercising.
Doug:	6. _____
John:	The food in fast-food restaurants is disgusting.
Doug:	7. _____

1 Frame 2

Read this conversation, then complete Doug's responses below in a similar way:

John: Oh my God! Your furniture is so old!

Doug: *Well, just because it's old doesn't mean* it's no good.

John: Your salary is so small!

Doug: *Well, just because I don't make a lot of money doesn't mean* I'm not happy.

John: Are you going to wear that tonight? You're out of fashion.

Doug: *Well, just because I'm not trendy like you doesn't mean* I don't look good.

John: You don't have E-mail? Where do you come from?

Doug: 1. _____

John: You've never been to America? You must be the only one.

Doug: 2. _____

John: You went to St. Mary's University? I've never hear of it.

Doug: 3. _____

John: Your wife is ugly.

Doug: 4. _____

John: You mean you don't speak French? I'm shocked.

Doug: 5. _____

John: You're too old to go out dancing.

Doug: 6. _____

John: You can't come dancing with us – you're married.

Doug: 7. _____

2 Pair Debate

Work in pairs. Separately, make a list of all the good and bad things about a topic. For example, country life vs. city life

Partner 1:   *Country life is boring.*

Partner 2:   *Well, it may be boring, but at least it's safe. Besides, city life is dangerous.*

Partner 1:   *Well, just because it's dangerous doesn't mean it isn't fun. Besides, country life is . . . .*

Possible topics (choose one):

     a vacation in the USA *vs.* a vacation in Europe

     getting married *vs.* staying single

     driving *vs.* taking the bus

     keeping to the speed limit *vs.* driving fast

Use the boxes below to prepare some statements.

It may be		but at least	
Just because		doesn't mean	

Now you will do the same as in the Pair Debate, only this time between teams – Team 1 *vs.* Team 2. The topic is – *Which is better – writing a letter or making a call*? The team that has no more to say, loses.

LESSON 28

SURPRISE

Amazed Amy

Amy and Erik are at a family reunion. What is Amy like physically?

Amy:	Oh my God! Is that you, Erik? How did you ever get so fat!
Erik:	Oh, you know.
Amy:	(*Eating a piece of pizza*) I'm sorry. It's just that you caught me off-guard.
Erik:	I haven't been exercising much.
Amy:	I can't believe how different you look.[*Amy cuts a slice of chocolate cake.*]
Erik:	I've put on about sixty-five pounds.
Amy:	No way! You mean to tell me you've gained that much in ten years?
Erik:	Yeah. Amazing, isn't it?
Amy:	Of all the people in the world I never expected that you would get so big. (*She adds a little vanilla ice-cream to her cake.*)
Erik:	You must be stunned.
Amy:	A little. I mean, who would've guessed? Erik, the football captain . . . . fat. Never in my wildest dreams would I have imagined you so huge.
Erik:	And I can't get over how much thinner you're looking, Amy.
Amy:	Thank you. I'm down to 220 pounds now.

110

1 Matching

In pairs, make a phrase by matching the correct word(s). Try to do it without the dialogue.

1. I can't get	a. ever get like that?
2. It caught me	b. tell me you're still single?
3. Oh my	c. way!
4. I can't	d. off-guard.
5. How did you	e. believe it!
6. No	f. over how big your house is.
7. Do you mean to	g. God!
8. Of all the people in the	h. wildest dreams!
9. Who would've	i. world I never expected him to win.
10. Never in my	j. guessed?

2 Cloze

Use an expression to complete the sentences below.

Never in my wildest dreams	*I can't get over*	*No way!*
How did you	*off-guard*	*who would've guessed*
of all the	*I can't believe*	*Oh my God!*
mean to		

1. _____ . Did you hear what he said?
2. _____ ever find such a beautiful house?
3. The sad news really caught me _____ .
4. _____ you got married!
5. _____ . That's impossible!
6. You _____ tell me there's no more money?
7. I mean, _____ people in the world I never expected to see you here!
8. _____ the fact that you didn't write to me – or even call me.
9. I mean, _____ that he was married to the boss?
10. Delicious! _____ would I have imagined you could cook!

Now underline the phrases above that express surprise.

3 Pair Work

In the boxes below, add four more examples:

1. How did you ever

get so rich?

find the time to write so much?

think of such an original idea?

get such a great job?

_____

_____

_____

2. I can't get over how

well you play!

much you've grown!

cold it is outside!

delicious this is!

_____

_____

_____

3. I can't get over the fact that

it's already Christmas!

we lost!

nobody here speaks English!

you've never been to Europe!

_____

_____

_____

4 Dialogue Practice

In pairs, one person play Erik and the other, Amy. Try the following sequence:

1. Read the dialogue sitting down.
2. Read it while physically acting out the scene.
3. Do it without the script as much as possible, until you feel comfortable.
4. Do it for the class to see which pairs could win an Oscar.

5 Showing Surprise

Work in pairs. One person make the following remarks. The other make a surprised response by repeating a word or short phrase from what the first speaker says. The first one is done for you as an example.

1. The train left an hour ago.
   > An *hour ago*?
2. He gave me his car.
3. They were stolen.
4. They said it was a big job – it'll take at least three weeks.
5. In the end we were delayed 8 hours.
6. Kay's divorced.
7. It's actually more expensive.
8. I have to wake up at five-thirty.
9. The tickets are all sold out till Friday.
10. It was Gabriela who wrote a 20-page report in under three hours.

6 An Article in the Newspaper

Work in pairs. One person reads one of these articles and the other person reads the other one. *Without looking at the article you read*, tell your partner about it, and the listener will respond as in exercise 5.

Teacher Writes On 5-Year-Old's Face

Charleston, S.C. – A kindergarten teacher was suspended yesterday for writing "I'm short and stupid" with a marker on the face of a five-year-old girl who had forgotten to bring her homework on Wednesday.

School principal Marcel Bodemann said teacher Andrea Pimpel, who is white, used "extremely poor judgement."

An attorney for the student, who is black, called Pimpel a racist.

"The girl has learning problems," said Benjamin Berner, who wants Pimpel fired. "(Pimpel) as a teacher should be above racism."

Pimpel had no comment, but other students who were in the class said that after writing on the young girl's face, Pimpel laughed for at least five minutes, and made the five-year-old sit outside without lunch.

7-Year-Old Goes To Harvard

Cambridge, MA – Adela Robles doesn't want a Barbie doll for Christmas. She doesn't want a video game either. Young Adela wants a book on quantum physics and a new journal so she can continue writing poetry – in eight different languages.

"I'm so proud of her," said Casilda Sáez, Adela's mother. "When I was her age I didn't know what Harvard was."

Adela was already taking advanced mathematics classes when she was five, and could recite Shakespeare by the age of four.

Adela, who speaks German, Spanish, English, Italian, Russian, French, Chinese and Swahili with equal fluency, still likes to play with her friends, though.

"My favorite game is hide-and-seek," said the young scholar. "And I like ice-cream, too."

7 Showing Surprise 2

Another very useful way for a listener to show surprise is to repeat an auxiliary verb:

A: I'm not going to France after all.
B: *You're not?*

A: I can speak English, French and Chinese.
B: *You can?*

Now work in pairs. One person makes the following remarks and the other makes a surprised response using *You can? / You did? / He will?* **, etc.**

1. Cigarettes are going up again.   _____
2. I was the only woman at the meeting.   _____
3. Well, she lost her job, you know.   _____
4. I've been in jail.   _____
5. She has a tattoo of Mickey Mouse on her left arm.   _____
6. She says she can't come tonight.   _____
7. Guess who I met – Clint Eastwood.   _____
8. They didn't pass their exams.   _____
9 I think they should move.   _____
10. I'm not tired. I drank five cups of coffee this morning. _____

8 Student Biographies

Write the answers to the following questions – truthfully or not so truthfully, then tell your answers to your partner. Your partner answers using *You can?*, *You did?*, etc. For example:

A: I live in Seoul, but I'm really from Jupiter.
B: *You are?*

1. Where are you from?
2. How many languages do you speak?
3. What do you do?
4. How do you get to school?
5. Where do you live?
6. What's your favorite food?

9 Amazing Stories

Working in groups of three or four:
1. **Write down an amazing story. It should have many parts, and may be true or made up.**
2. **Tell the story to the others in your group.**
3. **The group reacts to your story using language learned in this unit.**
4. **Everyone in the group tells at least one story.**
For Example:

A: Did I ever tell you about the time I met Mel Gibson?
B: *No way!*
A: Yeah. He even shook my hand.
C: *He did? Oh my God!*
D: How did you ever get close to him?
A: I just said, 'Hello'.
B: *You mean to tell me you just* walked right up to him?
A: *Sure*, and then . . . .

CONVERSATION TABOOS 5

Shop Talk

One can never be too careful when talking about things in a store. People can be easily offended when discussing things like price and taste. This lesson deals with uncomfortable situations. Something is not right with this conversation. With a partner, decide what should be changed.

Shopkeeper: What do you need?
Customer: Nothing. Go away.
Shopkeeper: Fine.
Customer: Wait. How much for this leather coat?
Shopkeeper: One hundred thirty-five.
Customer: That's expensive!
Shopkeeper: Well, if you're poor I can show you something cheaper.
Customer: Do that.
Shopkeeper: We have this coat which is almost the same – but it's green and orange.
Customer: I don't want that! It's ugly!
Shopkeeper: Well, if you don't like it – goodbye.
Customer: Thanks for nothing.

With a partner, re-write the conversation. The phrases below will help you.

It's a little out of my price range.   *Thanks, anyway.*
I'm not sure I can spend that much right now.   *on a budget*
more moderately priced   *I'm just looking, thanks.*
not exactly what I had in mind

1 Dialogue Practice

When you finish re-writing the dialogue:

1. Ask the teacher for more suggestions.
2. Practice the new conversation with script.
3. Practice the new conversation without script.
4. Act out the new conversation.
5. Show the class.

2 Role Play

A: Hi. Are you still open?

B: Sorry. We're closed.

In pairs, decide:

1. Who is A?
2. Who is B?
3. Where are they? (i.e. A shop? What kind of shop?)
4. Make a complete conversation until you reach a solution.
5. Your teacher will ask you to show the class.

3 Who said it?

Some things below were said by a customer and the others by a shopkeeper. Decide who said what.

1. I'll be right with you. _____
2. How are you today? _____
3. Would you like to try that on? _____
4. Do you have it in a larger size? _____
5. Thanks for waiting. _____
6. What time do you close? _____
7. We're out of that size. _____
8. It's on sale. _____
9. I can order it for you if you like. _____
10. Will that be cash or credit card? _____
11. Do you carry men's shoes? _____
12. What's your return policy? _____
13. Would you like a receipt? _____
14. Will that be all for you today? _____
15. I'd appreciate that. _____

Now work out a new dialogue using all the phrases in this unit.

4 Discussion

1. Do you like shopping?
2. Do you enjoy window shopping?
3. Do you prefer to shop alone or with friends?
4. What kind of service do you prefer in shops?

COMPLIMENTS

Discuss

When is an appropriate time to pay a compliment? Can you think of a time when a compliment is inappropriate? Are compliments given a lot in your culture? Are they given mostly by men to women? Women to men? Women to women? Men to men?

Stepping Out

Ozzie, Simba, and André are meeting at a formal party. Complete their conversation using the responses at the top of the next page.

Ozzie: (1) _____

Simba: Thanks. And you must be André. Ozzie speaks very highly of you.

André: (2) _____

Ozzie: And if you don't mind my saying so, you look like you've lost weight.

Simba: (3) _____

André: Well, I don't mean to brag but women have been staring at me all evening.

Ozzie: (4) _____

André: Sure.

Simba: Well, Ozzie. You have outdone yourself this time. What an incredible suit.

Ozzie: You think so?

Simba: (5) _____

André: I think the blue in my tie matches my eyes perfectly . . . if I do say so myself.

Simba: (6) _____

André: Yes, but brown and blue make a great combination, don't you think?

a. Really...I'm not just saying that. I mean it.

b. Really? Well, I've heard many good things about you, too.

c. But your eyes are brown.

d. Wow! You look great!

e. I'll take that as a compliment.

f. It must be your nose. I mean that as a compliment.

1 Matching

In pairs, make a phrase by matching the correct word(s). Try to do it without the dialogue.

1. I don't mean to	a. it.
2. Ozzie speaks very	b. so?
3. I mean	c. things about you.
4. If you don't mind	d. highly of you.
5. You think	e. say so myself.
6. I'll take that	f. as a compliment.
7. I'm not just	g. brag but nobody cooks better than me.
8. I've heard good	h. my saying so, you look elegant.
9. I speak fluently, if I do	i. as a compliment.
10. I mean that	j. saying that.

2 Sorting

Sort the phrases above into the four categories below. Compare with a partner.

1. Giving a compliment: _____

_____

2. Receiving a compliment: _____

_____

3. Returning a compliment: _____

_____

4. Giving yourself a compliment: _____

_____

AND YOU CAN QUOTE ME ON THAT!

Speaking of compliments, here are some famous insults:

"He has not a single redeeming defect."

"I thought he was a young man of promise, but it appears he was a young man of promises."

"Would you buy a second-hand car from this man?"

"He was a legend in his own lunchtime."

"If you say, 'Hiya, Clark, how are you?' he's stuck for an answer!"

3 Pair Work

Choose the phrase that best completes the sentences below. Only one is possible for each.

1. This soup I made is delicious – _____ .
   - a. if I do say so myself.
   - b. I'll take that as a compliment.
   - c. I mean that as a compliment.
   - d. I'm not just saying that.

2. A: Daniela speaks very highly of you.
   - a. B: I'll take that as a compliment.
   - b. B: I've heard good things about you, too.
   - c. B: I mean that as a compliment.
   - d. B: I don't mean to brag.

3. A: Your house is absolutely beautiful.
   - a. B: I'm not just saying that.
   - b. B: I'll take that as a compliment.
   - c. B: I don't mean to brag.
   - d. B: You think so?

4. A: I admire you for what you're doing. Really. _____ .
   - a. I mean it.
   - b. I don't mean to brag.
   - c. You think so?
   - d. I'll take that as a compliment.

5. Every time I see you I feel happy – and _____ , either.
   - a. I mean it
   - b. I'm not just saying that
   - c. I mean that as a compliment
   - d. if I do say so myself

6. _____ people have told me that I have a perfect accent in English.
   - a. I'm not just saying that
   - b. If you don't mind my saying so
   - c. I don't mean to brag, but
   - d. I mean it

7. _____ , I think you have very good taste in clothes.
   - a. If you don't mind my saying so
   - b. I'm not just saying that
   - c. I don't mean to brag, but
   - d. If I do say so myself

8. A: You dance well for someone your age.
   - a. B: I'm not just saying that.
   - b. B: I'll take that as a compliment.
   - c. B: I mean that as a compliment.
   - d. B: If I do say so myself.

9. Your English is quite good. I thought you were American – _____ .
   - a. If you don't mind my saying so.
   - b. I mean it.
   - c. I'll take that as a compliment.
   - d. I mean that as a compliment.

4 Dialogue Practice

1. Practice the dialogue in groups of three.
2. Choose parts, then read the scene.
3. Act out the scene while reading the script.
4. Memorize the dialogue and perform it.

5 Discussion

Which of the following would you interpret as a compliment? Which would you interpret as an insult? Work with a partner. Write a "C" if you think it's a compliment, an "I" if you think it's an insult.

1. You remind me of my mother. ___
2. I would rather marry you than the most beautiful person in the world. ___
3. You're just like your father. ___
4. I think your house looks special. ___
5. You look like you've lost some weight. ___
6. Have you changed your hair? ___
7. You certainly have an appetite, don't you! ___
8. Is that a photograph of your daughter? Hmm, I love the frame! ___
9. Do you drive as well as you cook? ___
10. Your English is very good. I can almost hear no accent. ___
11. I never thought you could paint so well. ___
12. Thank you, no. The dinner was delicious, but I'm full. ___
13. You were accepted into Harvard? I can't believe it! ___
14. I could've chosen any man in the world, but I chose you. ___
15. You have a way of making people laugh. ___
16. I've never met anyone quite like you before. ___
17. I bet you were a perfect student in school. ___
18. You're so skinny! ___
19. I named my dog after you. ___
20. Your grey hair and wrinkles make you look distinguished. ___

1. **Do you like giving compliments?**
2. **Do you like receiving them?**
3. **Can you think of a compliment someone gave you that made you feel especially flattered?**

ANSWER KEY

Lesson 1

Exercise 1: 1–d, 2–e, 3–h, 4–a, 5–b, 6–j, 7–i, 8–c, 9–g, 10–f

Exercise 2: Remembering: 1,2,4,7,8,9   Forgetting: 3,5,6,10

Exercise 4: 1. Can you refresh my memory? 2. Come to think of it,... 3. It's on the tip of my tongue. 4. Now that you mention it,... 5. It's coming to me now. 6. I'm drawing a blank. 7. The name escapes me. 8. It slipped my mind. 9. For the life of me I can't remember. 10.That's right!

Lesson 2

Dialogue: 1–c, 2–e, 3–d, 4–a, 5–f, 6–b

Exercise 1: 1. I'm leaning toward Adela 2. I could go either way 3. I'm going to go with vanilla 4. I can't make up my mind 5. But then again, I also like tea 6. I have mixed feelings about them 7. I had my heart set on Mexican food 8. On second thought, I'll have the chocolate one 9. I'm debating whether to call her or write her a letter 10. On the plus side it's beautiful; on the minus side it's expensive 11. On the one hand we can go out; on the other hand we can stay home and watch TV

Exercise 3: 1–a, 2–d, 3–c, 4–a, 5–b, 6–a, 7–b, 8–a, 9–d, 10–b

Lesson 3

Exercise 1: 1–g, 2–e, 3–j, 4–d, 5–f, 6–b, 7–a, 8–i, 9–h, 10–c

Exercise 2: (Suggested answers) 1. good 2. warm/hot 3. polite 4. intelligent/smart/bright 5. fast 6. interesting 7. clean/neat/tidy 8. sanitary

Exercise 3: Suggested answers: 1. He has a nice personality. / Well, he's not exactly handsome. 2. Well, she's not very well-off. Well, she's not exactly rich. 3. He's kind of heavy-set. / Well, he's not exactly skinny. 4. Well, it's not very big. / Well, it's not exactly a mansion. / It's cozy. 5. Well, he's a little out of the ordinary. / Well, he's a bit eccentric. 6. Well, it's not very clean. / Well, it's not exactly spotless. 7. Well, she's not very fast. / Well, she's not exactly speedy. 8. Well, he's a bit on the slow side. / Well, he's not exactly a rocket scientist. / Well, he's no Einstein. 9. Well, she's not young anymore. / Well, she's not exactly in her prime. / She's in her later years. 10. Well, it could use a little tidying up. / Well, it's not what I would call clean. 11. We're having some problems right now. / I have some uncertainties regarding the future of this company. 12. It's not necessarily what I would have picked out. / I see you're into the 'retro' look.

Exercise 5: 1. Carnegie 2. Whitney Houston 3. Elizabeth Taylor

Lesson 4

Exercise 1: 1. line 2. question 3. bottom 4. down 5. comes 6. end 7. fact 8. key 9. talking 10. know 11. anything

Exercise 2: 1–c, 2–e, 3–a, 4–f, 5–g, 6–d, 7–b, 8–j, 9–i, 10–h, 11–k

Exercise 4: Role Play 1: "What we're really talking about here is your financial future", "The fact is people who finish college make much more money" **Role Play 2:** "When you get right down to it we are no better than other animals", "The key is to respect all living things", "It's a question of sacrifice. We must learn to live without meat." **Role Play 3:** "The bottom line is there is no one else who can do what I do as well as I do.", "In the end there is no other company I'd rather work for. I'd hate to leave." **Role Play 4:** "All I know is I love you and I want us to be together forever.", "It all comes down to how much you really want this relationship to grow.", "If you don't marry me, I won't have kids. And if I won't have kids, I don't want to be with you. That's the bottom line."

Lesson 5

Exercise 1: 1.Go for it 2. It's worth a try 3. It's now or never 4. It's a piece of cake 5. Give it your best shot 6. Just do the best you can 7. What have you got to lose? 8. You never know until you try 9. There's only one way to find out 10. What's the worst that could happen? 11. You stand as good a chance as anyone

Exercise 2: 1. for it 2. a chance as anyone 3. you try 4. or never 5. could happen 6. to find out 7. try 8. best shot 9. of cake 10. you can 11. to lose

Exercise 4: 1. Go for it. 2. Give it your best shot 3. You never know until you try/There's only one way to find out 4. You stand as good a chance as anyone. 5. What's the worse that could happen?/What have you got to lose? 6. It's worth a try. 7. It's now or never. 8. It's a piece of cake.

Unit 6

Exercise 1: (Suggested changes)

Teacher: Thank you for coming.
Parent: Sure. What seems to be the problem?
Teacher: I'm a bit disappointed in your daughter.
Parent: I'm not sure I understand.
Teacher: Well, I have some concerns about her study skills.
Parent: Can you give me an example?
Teacher: Her mathematics abilities are a little weak / need a little work.
Parent: Oh, I know it's not one of her strong points.
Teacher: And she's lacking a bit in spelling.
Parent: I see. Should I sit with her while she does her homework?
Teacher: It might not be a bad idea. Also, you might want to consider getting a tutor for her.
Parent: Thank you.
Teacher: Your daughter has a lot of potential, so I hope to see her improve.

Exercise 4: Teacher – 1, 6, 8, 12, 13

Lesson 7

Dialogue: 1–c, 2–f, 3–a, 4–g, 5–b, 6–d, 7–e
Exercise 1: 1. what do you call it 2. something to that effect 3. What's the word I'm looking for 4. For lack of a better word 5. I don't know what else to call it 6. I can't think of any other way to describe it 7. Or a couple...or what have you 8. you know, like a real couple 9. It's kind of hard to explain 10. How can I explain it

Exercise 2: 1–c, 2–a, 3–b, 4–c, 5–a, 6–c, 7–b, 8–c, 9–a, 10–a

Exercise 4: 1–a, 2–a, 3–b, 4–a, 5–b, 6–b, 7–b, 8–b, 9–b, 10–a, 11–a

Lesson 8

Exercise 1: 1. You could say that 2. If you only knew 3. I could tell you stories 4. Let's put it this way: it's big 5. That's nothing – you should see my other car 6. Suffice it to say it's not cheap 7. Let's just say he's not an Olympic athlete 8. It's warm out, to put it mildly 9. I've been to China, Japan, and Singapore – just to name a few 10. Just so you get an idea it's harder to learn than English 11. I've been to China, Japan, and Singapore – just to name a few 12. That's nothing – you should see my other car 13. Let's just say he's not an Olympic athlete 14. It's warm out, to put it mildly 15. Suffice it to say it's not cheap

Exercise 2: (natural-sounding): 1–a, 2–b, 3–a, 4–b, 5–a, 6–b. 7–a, 8–a

Lesson 9

Exercise 1: Suggested answers: 1. I've eaten some spicy food before, but Mexican has to be the spiciest. 2. I've visited some beautiful cities before, but San Francisco has to be the most. 3. I've been to some wonderful museums before, but The Louvre has to be the most. 4. I've learnt some difficult languages before, but English has to be the worst. 5. I've read some long books before, but The Grapes of Wrath has to be the longest. 6. I've seen some funny films before, but Fierce Creatures has to be the funniest. 7. I've had some bad days before, but today has to be the worst. 8. I've watched some brilliant TV shows before, but The X Files has to be the best.

Lesson 10

Dialogue: 1–e, 2–c, 3–a, 4–d, 5–h, 6–b, 7–g, 8–f

Exercise 1: 1–e, 2–c, 3–b, 4–a, 5–d, 6–j, 7–h, 8–g, 9–f, 10–i

Exercise 4: 1. we're talking 2. talk about 3. I'm telling you 4. was not your average 5. should've seen

Exercise 5: 1. I mean 2. (I mean) this 3. I mean 4. literally 5. (I mean) this 6. I mean, this, literally 7. I mean, literally 8. I mean, this

Lesson 11

Exercise 1: 1–i, 2–h, 3–c/d, 4–f, 5–k, 6–a, 7–j, 8–g, 9–b, 10–e, 11–d/c

Exercise 2: Meaning: Aren't you impressed?: Not bad, eh?, Is he (artistic), or what?, Isn't that something? **Meaning: I'm impressed:** I must admit, he does play the piano well, Quite impressive, How about that, Isn't that something, Can't beat that. **Meaning: I'm not impressed:** So what, Big deal, I've seen better, It's OK.

Exercise 3: Suggested answers: 1a. tasted 1b. had 1c. driven 1d. heard 1e. read 1f. flown 2. great/fantastic/wonderful/incredible 3. False 4. False 5. False 6. d is not possible 7. b and c are not possible 8. Depending on how it is pronounced, *It's OK* can mean the same as *That's all right* or *Don't worry.*

Lesson 12

Dialogue: Suggested changes:

Instructor:	OK. So, it's one-two-three, one-two-three. Got it?
Student:	Like this?
Instructor:	Not exactly.
Student:	How about now?
Instructor:	You've got the right idea. Watch again.
Student:	Like this?
Instructor:	You're on the right track. Don't worry — you'll get the hang of it.
Student:	Well, maybe if I practice enough I can dance like Fred Astaire.
Instructor:	Well, I don't know about that / I wouldn't go that far.

Exercise 2: Ones sure to get you dismissed: 3, 8, 10, and 13

Lesson 13

Dialogue: 1–b, 2–d, 3–h, 4–a, 5–g, 6–f, 7–e, 8–c

Exercise 1: 1. Typical 2. I thought so 3. As usual 4. It figures 5. Just as I thought 6. It never fails 7. I should've known 8. I was afraid of that 9. Jeff – who else? 10. I had a feeling he would 11. I'll bet he got a company car 12. Sure enough, he got the promotion

Exercise 2: 1. I should've 2. I had a feeling 3. Typical 4. who else 5. (It) never 6. Just as I thought 7. (It) figures 8. I'll bet 9. never fails 10. as usual 11. Sure 12. I thought

Exercise 3: 1–g, 2–e, 3–a, 4–d, 5–h, 6–c, 7–j, 8–b, 9–f, 10–i, 11–k

Lesson 14

Exercise 1: 1–e, 2–c, 3–a, 4–i, 5–b, 6–h, 7–j, 8–g, 9–f, 10–d

Exercise 2: 1. It's no big deal. 2. If it makes you feel any better... 3. Things always have a way of working themselves out. 4. If worst comes to worst... 5. Look at it this way:... 6. (You'll find a job) before you know it 7. You never know / Who knows, ... 8. Don't worry about it. 9. Don't let it get to you.

Exercise 5: 1–b, 2–a, 3–d, 4–c

Lesson 15

Exercise 1: Suggested answers: 1. Fired? I mean, I could see if I were late every day or something, but I've come on time nearly every Thursday. 2. A divorce? I mean, I could see if I were no good to you or something, but I've been home almost every night. 3. Lose weight? I mean, I could see if I were fat or something, but I only weigh 510 pounds 4. Fast? I mean, I could see if I were driving 200 miles an hour or something, but I'm only doing 180. 5. Fail? I mean, I could see if I were lazy or something, but I plan to study at least an hour before the exam 6. The heat? I mean, I could see if it were cold in here or something, but it's got to be at least 20 degrees Fahrenheit 7. Cut down? I mean, I could see if I smoked like a chimney or something, but I'm already down to 5 packs a day 8. Long? I mean, I could see if I had been on for a long time or something, but I just started talking an hour ago. 9. Too much? I mean, I could see if I were falling down drunk or something, but I fine just feel. 10. Sorry? I mean, I could see if I hurt him or something, but all I did was shave his head.

Lesson 16

Dialogue: 1–c, 2–d, 3–g, 4–b, 5–e, 6–a, 7–f

Exercise 1: 1–c, 2–e, 3–g, 4–h, 5–d, 6–i, 7–a, 8–j, 9–f, 10–b

Exercise 2: 1. safe with me 2. a secret 3. from me 4. a little secret 5. around 6. any names
7. you and me 8. record 9. world to know 10. gets out

Exercise 3: 1–a, 2–a, 3–c, 4–d, 5–a, 6–c, 7–d, 8–d, 9–a, 10–c

Exercise 5: Sample dialogue:

Interviewer:	So, what can you tell us about Mr. Angelino's life?
Housekeeper:	Well, you didn't hear this from me, but he has been having a secret relationship with a beautiful young woman.
Interviewer:	Really? For how long?
Housekeeper:	About ten years.Interviewer: And, what was her name?
Housekeeper:	I know she works with him, but I won't mention any names.
Interviewer:	I see. What else can you tell us about him?
Housekeeper:	Well, can you keep a secret?
Interviewer:	Sure.
Housekeeper:	Johnny snores at night
Interviewer:	Interesting. Anything else?
Housekeeper:	Well, I don't want the whole world to know, but he loves to read comic books. Also, I'll let you in on a little secret: Johnny has never been to acting school, and, off the record, he only gets big roles because of the important people he's connected with.
Interviewer:	Very interesting. Anything else you'd like to add?
Housekeeper:	Well, I don't want this to get around, but Johnny also likes to sing – but just between you and me, I think he only sounds good in the shower.
Interviewer:	Thank you so much for your time.
Housekeeper:	Remember: if word gets out that I've told you all this I'm fired.
Interviewer:	Don't worry, ma'am – your secret's safe with me.

Lesson 17

Exercise 1: 1. Good one, Eddie. 2. Me and my big mouth. 3. What was I thinking?
4. I should've known better 5. What is it with me and names today? 6. I can't believe what an idiot I am. 7. It's not like me to forget my keys. 8. Serves me right for ordering the lobster.
9. I guess that's what I get for being nice. 10. What possessed me to marry him I'll never know.

Exercise 2: 1–b, 2–a, 3–a, 4–a, 5–b, 6–b, 7–a, 8–b, 9–a, 10–b, 11–b

Lesson 18

Exercise 1: Suggested changes:

Victim 1:	So then I told him, I said, "You have no business . . . ."
Stranger:	Excuse me. Not to interrupt, but I couldn't help overhearing you speaking in English. I hate to be nosy, but . . . are you from England?
Victim 2:	No, we're not, actually.
Stranger:	Well, then . . .where are you from, if you don't mind my asking.
Victim 1&2:	New Zealand.
Stranger:	Oh. I couldn't help noticing you have cameras. I take it you're on holiday.
Victim 1:	Yes, we are, actually.

Stranger:	For how long, if you don't mind my asking.		
Victim 2:	One week.		
Stranger:	I don't mean to be nosy, but . . . why so short?		
Victim 1:	No time.		
Stranger:	Oh, I see. It's really none of my business, but . . . are you married?		
Victim 1&2:	Yes, we are, actually.		
Stranger:	Just out of curiosity, do you have a big house in New Zealand?		
Victim 2:	No, we don't. Why do you ask?		
Stranger:	Oh. Well, I was just wondering if I could come visit some time.		

Exercise 3: Ones which are probably rude: 1, 2, 7, 8, 9, 10, 15

Note: Number 15 should be used only in extreme circumstances or when obviously joking! For example:

A: Will you ever forgive me for stealing your money?

B: *Yeah, when hell freezes over*!

Lesson 19

Exercise 1: A: 1–c, 2–d, 3–b, 4–a, 5–e;   B: 1–g, 2–i, 3–f, 4–j, 5–h

Exercise 3: 1–c, 2–b, 3–a, 4–b, 5–a, 6–a, 7–c, 8–a, 9–a, 10–a

Lesson 20

Exercise 1: 1. It's getting there. 2. That's more like it. 3. It's going downhill. 4. It's come a long way. 5. It's got a long way to go. 6. What's this world coming to? 7. It's a step in the right direction. 8. It's just one thing after another. 9. It's getting to the point where even a degree won't help. 10. The way things are going our children won't be able to go to college.

Exercise 2: Phrases which mean getting better: 1, 2, 4, 5, 7; Phrase which mean getting worse: 3, 6, 8, 9, 10

Exercise 3: 1. to be going downhill 2. What's this world coming to? 3. it's getting to the point where 4. has come a long way 5. the way things are going (Note: *it's getting to the point where* is followed by a verb in the present tense, whereas *the way things are going* is followed by verbs which have a future or conditional meaning).

Exercise 4: 1. we've got a long way to go 2. just one thing after another 3. a step in the right direction 4. it's getting there 5. that's more like it

Lesson 21

Exercise 1: Different answers are possible. Here are some suggestions:

What good is having	a guitar	if you don't	play it?
What good is having	a swimming pool	if you don't	use it?
What good is having	a leather sofa	if you don't	use it?
What good is having	a collection of CD's	if you don't	listen to them?
What good is having	three nephews	if you don't	spend time with them?
What good is having	a video collection	if you don't	watch them?
What good is having	expensive wine	if you don't	drink it?
What good is having	fantastic books	if you don't	read them?
What good is having	an enormous bed	if you don't	sleep in it?
What good is having	a loving husband	if you don't	live with him?

| What good is having | designer clothes | if you don't | wear them? |
| What good is having | a beautiful garden | if you don't | take care of it? |

Lesson 22

Exercise 1: 1. I have no idea 2. Your guess is as good as mine 3. It's anyone's guess 4. Who knows? 5. There's no telling 6. Who's to say 7. You got me 8. Good question 9. Don't ask me 10. How should I know?

Exercise 3: 1. Although English is the most widely-spoken language in the United States, there is no real 'official' language. 2. John Lennon, Paul McCartney, George Harrison, and Ringo Starr 3. Baseball and Cricket 4. Unidentified Flying Object 5. Canada, USA, England, Scotland, Ireland, South Africa, Australia, New Zealand 6. Father Christmas or Santa Claus 7. Fifty 8. The Great Wall of China 9. Romeo and Juliet, Love's Labours' Lost, Twelfth Night, King Lear, Macbeth, Hamlet, A Midsummer Night's Dream, As You Like It, Othello, The Tempest, among others 10. They both contain one gallon 11. Seven: North America, South America, Europe, Asia, Africa, Australia and Antarctica 12. In San Francisco 13. Kyoto 14. In Buenos Aires, Argentina 15. A frown

Lesson 23

Exercise 1: 1. We're 2. I'd 3. are 4. guess is 5. It, that 6. it's hard to 7. Knowing 8. go as far as to say 9. If I had to take a guess 10. Just off the top of my head

Exercise 2: 1. True 2. c 3. a 4. Knowing (these German imports) 5. (not possible) b, c 6. Best answer: I would say you're about thirty-six.

Exercise 4: 1–F, 2–F, 3–T, 4–T, 5–F, 6–F, 7–F, 8–F, 9–T, 10–F, 11–F, 12–T

Exercise 5: 1. feeling 2. bones 3. intuition 4. sixth 5. hunch

Lesson 24

Exercise 1: Suggested changes:

Boss: Clint! Have you finished that report?

Clint: I haven't got around to it yet.

Boss: When do you think it will be done?

Clint: Should be any day now.

Boss: Why is it taking so long?

Clint: It's a long story.

Boss: And the proposal?

Clint: I'm working on it.

Boss: When can you have it finished?

Clint: It may take a while.

Boss: Also, I would like you to make plans for a new building by tomorrow.

Clint: I'll see what I can do.

Boss: How long will it take?

Clint: I'll do the best I can. It shouldn't be long.

Lesson 25

Exercise 1: 1. but don't quote me on that 2. I'm no expert, but 3. I'm just going by what they've told me 4. From what I understand, 5. From what I gather, 6. but I could be wrong 7. as far as I know 8. from what I hear 9. my understanding was 10. the way I understand... 11. The way I 12. As far 13. From what 14. going by 15. expert 16. wrong 17. I hear 18. understanding 19. gather 20. quote me

Exercise 2: 1. hear, understand, gather, see, am told, remember 2. but don't quote me on that 3. but (this word is essential to the phrase because the person is saying that their opinion is valuable regardless of their (lack of) expertise 4. True 5. 'as long as' means 'only if X happens'. For example: 'OK, I'll go out to dinner with you as long as it's not too expensive'. 6. a

Exercise 4: 1. A: I want to go skiing this weekend. (Apparently) There's (apparently) been a lot of snow (apparently). B: Yeah, but (apparently) it's (apparently) not very good (apparently). A: (Apparently) They've (apparently) put some artificial snow there now (apparently). B: Oh, I didn't know that. 2. A: Have you seen Marcel around lately? B: (Apparently) He's (apparently) been sick (apparently). A: Oh, really? (Apparently) There's (apparently) something going around (apparently). B: Yeah, (apparently) some kind of flu (apparently). 3. A: What do you know about the TOEFL exam? B: (Apparently) It's (apparently) very difficult (apparently). A: (Apparently) You (apparently) have to get a minimum score of 550 (apparently). B: (Apparently) The listening part is (apparently) the most difficult (apparently).

Lesson 26

Exercise 1: 1–d, 2–h, 3–f, 4–j, 5–i, 6–a, 7–b, 8–e, 9–g, 10–c 11. Five down and two to go 12. Time's up. 13. As usual, we'll probably end up going back to his place. 14. So much for the millionaire lifestyle 15. On that note, I'll say goodbye.

Exercise 2: Suggested answers: 1. a person receiving a haircut 2. a wife to her husband/a mother to her son 3. a customer at a bakery 4. someone who has been holding a barbecue 5. a teacher 6. a person holding a meeting 7. a couple of painters 8. the host of a television show 9. expecting parents 10. a server at a restaurant

Exercise 3: 1. *Let's get this over with* is used before beginning the action and *Let's call it quits* when one has already begun. 2. It's probably raining (or worse) 3. drunk; throwing it away 4. Three down and one to go! 5. Time's up! 6. "On that note, why don't we break for lunch and come back in an hour." 7. That should just about do it 8. that's it for 9. True

Exercise 6: 1–g, 2–e, 3–i, 4–h, 5–b, 6–j, 7–a, 8–d, 9–c, 10–f

Lesson 27

Self Defense: Suggested answers: 1. They may be ugly, but at least they last 2. It may not be very nice, but at least it's warm 3. I may be old, but at least I'm not boring 4. I may be boring, but at least I'm not stupid like you 5. They may be dirty, but at least they come on time 6. I may spend too much time exercising, but at least I look healthy 7. It may be disgusting, but at least it's cheap

Exercise 1: Suggested answers: 1. Well, just because I don't have E-mail doesn't mean I'm behind the times 2. Well, just because I haven't been to America doesn't mean I'm not well-traveled 3. Well, just because you've never heard of it doesn't mean it isn't good

4. Well, just because she's ugly doesn't mean we have a bad marriage 5. Well, just because I don't speak French doesn't mean I'm not multi-lingual 6. Well, just because I'm old doesn't mean I can't put you to shame on the dance floor 7. Well, just because you're on a diet doesn't mean you can't look at the menu...if you know what I mean.

Lesson 28

Exercise 1: 1–f, 2–d, 3–g, 4–e, 5–a, 6–c, 7–b, 8–i, 9–j, 10–h

Exercise 2: 1. Oh my god! 2. How did you 3. off-guard 4. I can't believe 5. No way! 6. mean to 7. of all the 8. I can't get over 9. who would've guessed 10. Never in my wildest dreams

Exercise 5: Suggested answers: 2. (his) car? 3. Stolen? 4. Three weeks? 5. 8 hours? 6. Divorced? 7. More expensive? 8. Five-thirty? 9. Sold out?/Till Friday? 10. Gabriela?/A 20-page report?/Three hours?

Exercise 7: 1. They are? 2. You were? 3. She did? 4. You have? 5. She does? 6. She can't? 7. You did? 8. They didn't? 9. You do?/They should? 10. You're not?/You did?

Lesson 29

Suggested changes:

Shopkeeper:	May I help you?
Customer:	I'm just looking, thanks.
Shopkeeper:	Fine.
Customer:	Excuse me. How much is this leather coat?
Shopkeeper:	One hundred thirty-five.
Customer:	It's a little out of my price-range. I'm not sure I can spend that much right now.
Shopkeeper:	Well, if you're on a budget, I can show you something more moderately priced.
Customer:	That'd be great.
Shopkeeper:	We have this coat which is almost the same – but it's green and orange.
Customer:	It's not exactly what I had in mind, to be honest.
Shopkeeper:	Sorry. That's all we have in stock right now.
Customer:	OK. Thanks, anyway.

Exercise 3: Customer: 4, 6, 11, 12, 15; Shopkeeper: 1, 2, 3, 5, 7, 8, 9, 10, 13, 14

Lesson 30

Dialogue: 1–d, 2–b, 3–e, 4–f, 5–a, 6–c

Exercise 1: 1–g, 2–d, 3–a, 4–h, 5–b, 6–f, 7–j, 8–c, 9–e, 10–i

Exercise 2: 1. (Ozzie) speaks very highly of you; I mean it; If you don't mind my saying so,...; I'm not just saying that; I've heard good things about you; I mean that as a compliment 2. You think so?; I'll take that as a compliment 3. I've heard good things about you, too; (or simply, "[Thanks] You, too.") 4. I don't mean to brag, but...; ...if I do say so myself

Exercise 3: 1–a, 2–b, 3–d, 4–a, 5–b, 6–c, 7–a, 8–b, 9–d